Pelican Books
Creativity in Industry

G000240818

P. R. Whitfield graduated from London University with
degrees in Electrical Engineering and Psychology. After
serving in the army in the Second World War, he began
his career as an electrical engineer with the British
Electricity Authority. In 1955, he joined the Associated
Octel Company to carry out special electrical investigation
work, and in 1960 moved to Imperial Chemical Industries.
He is now an internal consultant in Organization
Development with the Mond Division of ICI, and he has
been a member of the Council of Engineering Institution's
Committee on Creativity and Innovation since its
formation in 1967. In 1970 he received a Council of
Engineering Institution's Senior Visiting Fellowship at
Liverpool University to be associated with a research
project on innovation in industry. P. R. Whitfield is
married, with three children, and among his interests are
sailing, boat building, music and industrial archaeology.

P. R. Whitfield

Creativity in Industry

Penguin Books

Penguin Books Ltd,
Harmondsworth, Middlesex, England
Penguin Books Inc.,
7110 Ambassador Road, Baltimore, Maryland 21207, U.S.A.
Penguin Books Australia Ltd,
Ringwood, Victoria, Australia
Penguin Books Canada Ltd,
41 Steelcase Road West, Markham, Ontario, Canada
Penguin Books (N.Z.) Ltd,
182–190 Wairau Road, Auckland 10, New Zealand

First published 1975
Copyright © P. R. Whitfield, 1975

Made and printed in Great Britain by
Richard Clay (The Chaucer Press) Ltd
Bungay, Suffolk
Set in Monotype Times

Contents

1 What are Creativity and Innovation?

This book is about technological innovation, mainly as it concerns us as individuals and the small groups in which we work. At this level it looks at the nature of innovation and how it can be improved, at people who innovate and at the consequences of innovation both near and far. So we shall consider innovation as a process, examine its component parts and consider it as part of society in general, in all its complexity.

What do we mean by innovation? The pen I write with is one of the felt-tip variety. It is a product which has gone through a long process, including somebody's bright idea of storing ink in a length of porous fibre and sharpening the end to write with, and many complicated technical and commercial steps to develop the idea and present a useful and desirable article to the public. This is an example of an innovation – the development of a creative idea into a finished article (or process or system since, from the start, we are concerned with more than just 'things' as innovations).

We have just used the word 'creative' to describe the idea that is to be developed into an innovation, and in doing so have indicated something special, a quality which is also implied in words like novelty, inspiration, ingenuity, originality, invention, genius and imagination. All these words seem to have the quality of creativity in common, though separately describing an idea, the mental activity which forms it or the ability of the person to carry out this activity. Let us consider in turn these three ways of looking at creativity.

Creativity applied to the product of mental activity may be defined in terms of unexpectedly appropriate combinations or associations of ideas. The nineteenth-century writer H. L. Mansel says: 'We can think of creation only as a change in the condition of that which already exists.' Koestler (1964) sees it as 'a new synthesis of previously unconnected matrices of thought'. Joshua Reynolds agrees but applies his definition to the more specific but synonymous 'invention': 'Invention is little more than new combinations of those images which have been previously gathered and deposited in the memory. Nothing can be made of nothing; he who has laid up no material can produce no combinations.'

Something of the quality of these new syntheses or combinations can be gained by considering the unexpectedness and sheer novelty of the result, its appropriateness, completeness, simplicity, neatness and 'intellectual distance' between elements of the new combinations. We shall come to the assessment of quality a little later, but for the moment let us dwell on the idea that whatever is created is derived from what is already there. A wall is no more than the combination of the number, shape and texture of the bricks we possess and can only be built up brick upon brick: we cannot build in mid-air. Music is merely the arrangement of sounds into a sequence; sculpture the physical shaping of inanimate matter. What such combinations convey to other people artistically, of course, is another matter.

'Association of ideas' is a phenomenon known to everyone: one idea comes to mind and evokes others having some linkage with it. Think of food and all sorts of images crowd in: meals we have had, special dishes we enjoy, hunger, people, places. Each association, though unique to us individually in the circumstances of its formation, would cause little surprise to other people because the idea of food to them is accompanied by a similar cluster of memories and feelings. But if the concept 'food' is somehow associated with the apparently unconnected concept 'X-rays' we just might get the creative idea of irradiating food with X-rays to kill bacteria and prolong its edible life. There is nothing new in any of the concepts used: food, X-rays, irradiation, sterilization or edibility; but there is something new in the combination.

To regard creativity as a simple though perhaps very significant recombination of discrete elements would be rather too atomistic. Our knowledge, experience and behaviour seem to be more in the form of organized patterns than a collection of separate bits. Change in one part of a pattern can alter the whole, just as a simple stroke of the brush can change the meaning of a whole picture. Creativity from this angle is a sudden change in the whole field of perception in which the new pattern represents a fresh insight or solution to a problem.

This approach gives a lead to the second way of looking at creativity: as a mental activity. Wertheimer (1945) describes it as 'an action that produces a new idea or "insight" fully formed; it comes to the individual in a flash'. He sees the process beginning as a focusing on one part of the whole field of awareness which, however, is not isolated from the rest. This gives a deepening appreciation of the structure of the field and the meaning, grouping and organization of the items in it, followed by changes and reorganizations until the gaps and unresolved difficulties are clarified. Harmony is restored by an instantaneous restructuring of the field, a flash of inspiration resolving the disequilibrium previously present.

Though creativity seen in this way may be a purely intellectual activity, its effect seems to spill over into our feelings to give that 'Eureka' experience of pleasure and emotional release – the 'exhilaration, glow and elation of the "aha" experience', in the words of MacKinnon (1961). Koestler (1964), too, speaks of the creative act operating on more than one plane: ' . . . a double minded, transitory state of unstable equilibrium where the balance of both emotion and thought is disturbed'. J. S. Bruner (1962) uses the 'feel' of the situation as a definition of creativity: 'An act that produces effective surprise.' And for Gordon (1961) it is a predictor: 'When the goal of invention is achieved, it is preceded, signalled and accompanied by a pleasurable mental excitement. This pleasurable excitement itself (the feeling of being on the right track) is a purposeful psychological state, recognized unconsciously as an indicator of the direction to take.'

As a mental activity, the moment of creation appears to be largely outside our conscious control, although it is more likely to be stimulated when we have become immersed in a subject. A burning desire to find a solution, concentration, gathering and marshalling of facts, and striving for completion by reaching out for still vague ideas are all activities we can feel and largely control at a conscious level. They mobilize and direct energy to finding a solution, but they are really only precursors to the act of creation, which seems to have a quality of spontaneity making it difficult to track and explain.

A hint of the process at work when thinking is uncoupled from full conscious control is given by Henle (1962): 'The creative solution, the creative idea, is one in which the individual achieves by freeing himself from his own conceptual system and by which he sees in a deeper or comprehensive or clearer way the structure of the situation he is trying to understand.' A century and more ago, the poet Samuel Taylor Coleridge was describing his experience as 'Facts which sank at intervals out of conscious recollection drew together beneath the surface through the almost chemical affinities of common elements.' And Koestler (1964) suggests that there is a continuous traffic between the conscious and the unconscious. Knowledge and experience, patterns of behaviour and skill when fully mastered are all passed down to the unconscious where they remain, to surface again in 'small fluctuating pulses . . . which sustain the dynamic balance of the mind', and in the rare sudden surges of creativity, which may lead to a restructuring of the whole mental landscape. Such restructuring takes place when 'thinking aside'; when rational control of thinking is relinquished 'in favour of the codes which govern the underground games of the mind'.

The role of the unconscious, however, is disputed by Kubie (1958). To him both the conscious and the unconscious are rigid and do not allow for fantasy or imaginative thinking. 'The preconscious system' (that is, the intermediate region between the conscious and the unconscious whose contents can easily be brought into consciousness: the seat of the memory) 'is the essential ingredient of creativity and unless preconsciousness can bloom freely there can be no creativity.'

Harding (1967) suggests that the flash of inspiration often associated with scientific and engineering problems comes when the scientist tries to rest by turning away from his problem. When thinking or doing something else the solution suddenly comes to him. The problem has not really been entirely forgotten, Harding argues, but merely set aside and held in the 'corner of the mind's eye while focusing on something else'. This not only rests the brain, but keeps it ready to catch anything which will help in leading to a solution.

Interesting as they are in suggesting where creative activity occurs, these observations offer little help in describing the actual process. We do not know what goes on at the neurone level, how nerve cells make their individual contribution or act together to form new patterns and insights. But there does seem to be a basic organizing and re-organizing activity going on all the time within the mind. Sinnott (1959) draws the parallel between the living organism which 'pulls together random, formless stuff into the patterned system of structure and function in the body' and the unconscious mind which 'seems to select and arrange and correlate these ideas and images into a pattern . . . it seems clear that mind, or whatever its physical correlate may be, when confronted with the throng of unassociated stimuli pouring into it from the organs of sense, is able to organize them, largely without conscious effort, into patterns . . . The patterns it makes are new things, not repetitions of something in the past.' Thus, to Sinnott, organization at the unconscious level is continuous and natural, and creativity but a special example by virtue of its dramatic and conspicuous effect.

Structuring in the form of dreams and daydreams to express wish-fulfilment was attributed to the unconscious by Freud, who places great emphasis on the dynamic force exerted by this part of the mind. Creativity to him was 'a substitute, a means of running from hardships in order to achieve some degree, limited at times, of satisfaction' (Mackler and Shontz, 1965).

If the unconscious has this function of creating new patterns out of the old, then at the conscious level we must pay the price of constant re-adjustment. 'The act of discovery,' observes Koestler (1964), 'actually has a destructive and a constructive aspect. It must disrupt rigid patterns of mental organization to achieve the new synthesis.' Abercrombie (1971) has a similar view: ' . . . it demands a coming to terms with destruction: by definition the more brilliant the invention, the newer it is, the deeper and more widespread are the changes in the old that it demands . . . to accept that the world is round when you'd thought it flat . . . to accept such ideas at the times when they were revolutionary, must have involved a wholesale modification of vast complexes of associated ideas, attitudes and habits of thinking.'

Turning now to the third view of creativity – as an ability, part of a person's intellectual makeup which is identifiable, like blue eyes or red hair – we are brought back to a consideration of creativity as a process because an ability can really only be described in terms of the power to perform a mental or physical act. Nevertheless, it is worth examining some of the notions which have been put forward to describe the structure of the mind in terms of mental abilities and the nature of intelligent behaviour to see where creativity fits in with these hypotheses.

Intelligent behaviour has been variously described as the forming of associations, the integration and synthesis of ideas, showing good judgement and reasoning, adjusting to new situations, abstract thinking, and constructive thinking directed to the attainment of some end. There are many other descriptions. Theories of intelligence include those of Cattell (1963), who suggests that general intelligence is a function of two separate but correlated factors: 'crystallized intelligence', which shows itself in situations requiring learned habits of thinking, and 'fluid intelligence', needed in situations where existing patterns of cognitive skill are inadequate; and of Hebb (1949), who also distinguishes two types of intelligence: 'intelligence A', which is 'an innate potential, the capacity for development, a fully innate property that amounts to the possession of a good brain and a good neural metabolism', and 'intelligence B', which is the functioning of the brain at any given time. Piaget sees intelligence as the quality of adaptation to the environment in order to maintain equilibrium. This is achieved by the processes of mental assimilation – incorporating changes in the environment into existing personal 'schema' – and accommodation – modifying these schema to fit the realities of the environment. 'Schema' is a concept of Piaget's used to describe a behaviour sequence, for example the schema of grasping or sight; also a cognitive structure, an organized disposition to behave in this way; and a psychological organ functionally equivalent to a physiological organ for incorporating reality into the intellectual repertoire (Flavell, 1963).

In these definitions and theories intelligence is presented as the mediator between the individual and the outside world. To be successful it has to enable him to comprehend, remember, analyse and make logical associations, to deduce and evaluate, and to adapt, imagine, integrate and synthesize according to the circumstances of the situation. Many tests have been devised to isolate and measure the basic factors which make up this complex capacity. Thurstone (1941), for instance, obtained seven relatively independent factors:

Verbal comprehension: ability to define and understand words, make verbal analogies, match proverbs, reason verbally.

Word fluency: ability to think rapidly in words, solve anagrams and make rhymes.

Number: ability to do arithmetic problems with speed and accuracy.

Space: ability to visualize relationships and to draw from memory, to manipulate and move parts.

Memory: ability to memorize and recall.

Perception: ability to group visual details and compare objects quickly and correctly.

Reasoning: ability to find rules, principles or concepts for understanding or solving problems.

These factors were based on the results of many tests given to schoolchildren. Such tests were constructed in such a way that there was only one right answer to each question; for instance given the problem 'If $7\frac{1}{2}$ lb. of tea cost £3, what will $4\frac{1}{2}$ lb. cost?' the answer can only be £1·80; or 'Dog is to barks as lion is to —— (squeals, prowls, roars, leaps)' is only correct when the word 'roars' is selected. Questions such as 'Give as many uses as possible for a brick' cannot be scored right or wrong and were excluded from the type of test used by Thurstone. Although these tests, and others like them, were called 'intelligence' tests they specifically left out questions whose answers required some subjective assessment of novelty, and the essential nature of creative thinking was never examined.

However, from our discussion on intelligence itself, the ability to deal with novelty cannot be ignored. Tests designed to measure the power and uniqueness of association in verbal and visual forms have been devised by Getzels and Jackson (1962) (devise mathematical problems; detect geometric figures embedded in another pattern; compare endings for fables, etc.), and by Wallach and Kogan (1965) (generate possible instances of a class concept such as 'round things', or 'things that move on wheels'; propose similarities between two objects such as 'tram' and 'tractor'; think of possible interpretations or meanings for given abstract visual patterns, etc.). These tests do seem to some extent to isolate individual differences in creative thinking (although Hudson (1966) would prefer to call it only a measure of 'divergent thinking'), as distinct from 'intelligence', claimed to be assessed by the tests of Thurstone and others. Wallach and Kogan indeed claim to have found four types of pairings in children: high creativity, high intelligence; high creativity, low intelligence; low creativity, high intelligence; and low creativity, low intelligence. Support for the non-correlation between intelligence, as measured by I Q tests, and creativity comes from MacKinnon (1962), who tested scientists, architects and writers whose creative abilities were acknowledged by their peers. He concludes: 'It is clear, however, that above a certain required minimum level of intelligence which varies from field to field and in some instances may be surprisingly low, being more 'intelligent' does not guarantee a corresponding increase in creativeness. It is just not true that the more intelligent person is necessarily the more creative one.' It might be added that a high I Q is not an infallible predictor of eminence in any field, except that of passing I Q tests! The term 'genius' does not apply to such a person, but to him whose exalted intellectual power lies in the region of his extraordinarily imaginative and creative capacity.

Many theories have been proposed to describe the structure of the mind when engaged on different types of tasks. Spearman (1927) compared the performance of schoolchildren in various tests with their school achievements and by a process called factor analysis calculated how much correlation there was between all the material. His results led him to conclude that intelligence was made up of a general ability, 'g', which contributed to all tests, and a number of specialized abilities which were active in groups of allied activities. Other British psychologists presented a modified theory which retained the general ability 'g' but replaced the specific factors with group factors each of which contributed in differing degrees to a number of tests. These group factors were labelled 'verbal', 'arithmetic', 'spatial', etc. Thurstone, whom we have mentioned before, disagreed with the existence of the general ability and proposed instead the seven primary group factors, verbal comprehension, word fluency, etc., described on page 13.

Guilford (1959) has sought to give a much more comprehensive description of the working of the mind, including the intellectual activities concerned with creativity. He proposes a theory of the intellect in which intellectual functioning can be described in terms of 'operations', 'contents' (what these operate on) and 'products' (what they produce). Each of these basic components has a number of variations on the same theme: 'operations' include the abilities of cognition, memory, divergent thinking, convergent thinking and evaluation; 'content' may be figural, symbolic, semantic or behavioural; and 'products' may be in the form of units, classes, relations, systems, transformations or implications. He has presented a three-dimensional model (Fig. 1) showing these components and their variations which is useful for linking them together to identify different kinds of mental behaviour.

In this model there are 120 'boxes', each linking an operation, a content and a product, and representing a different mental activity. For instance, the box (shown shaded) linking the operation 'cognition', the content 'figural' and the product 'implication' represents an activity such as the visual exploration of several courses of action to select the best one, as in, say, thinking ahead several moves in a game of chess. The box at the intersection of the divergent thinking operation, figural content and transformation product, represents an activity such as looking for other ways of solving a problem which can be perceived or imagined in some physical form and ending with a novel solution. An example of this kind of activity is given when the conventional way of looking at an alternating-current motor as a stationary cylindrical coil with an electromagnet rotating inside it is

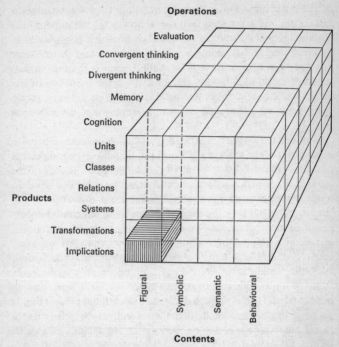

Fig. 1. Guilford's 'structure of the intellect'.

abandoned, and the roles are reversed to give the idea of a stationary electromagnet and a moving coil; and when at the same time the coil is opened out flat instead of remaining cylindrical, we get the novel idea of the linear induction motor.

Guilford (1963) suggests that the most conspicuous operation in creativity is divergent thinking, although many other intellectual abilities can play a part in the creative person's work. Divergent thinking, which may be regarded metaphorically as the mind's eye switching to its wide-angled lens to expand the field of view, can be a crucial factor in extending the opportunities for seeing a problem in a different perspective and discovering previously unthought-of solutions. But convergent thinking, the mind's zoom lens which brings selected areas into close detail and excludes the rest of the field, is important too for problem definition. In the evaluation category comes the factor of sensitivity to problems, and this, together with the other two operations, cognition and memory, must contribute to creative behaviour.

Of the six 'products', transformations are the most important. These represent some kind of change of existing information such as a restructuring or a reinterpretation. Other products also have some relevance. Grouping bits of information into a class, seeing relationships between units of information, organizing units into systems and drawing inferences or conclusions from the extrapolation of information – all have some characteristic which we would recognize as creative.

To Guilford, then, many aspects of the human intellect contribute to a man's creativity, and he has illustrated them by examples and devised tests to isolate them one from another. His list includes:

sensitivity to problems (shown, for instance, by people who can readily see defects in existing systems or machines);

fluency of thinking (fertility of ideas in producing solutions to a given problem, or, in the narrower area of verbal fluency, in producing words containing a specified letter or letters, thinking up synonyms for a given word, or juxtaposing words to form a sentence);

flexibility of thinking (the ability to take a fresh approach to a problem without being too constrained by existing solutions and thinking habits);

originality (thinking of ideas or solutions which not many other people would suggest);

redefinition (seeing familiar objects or concepts in a fresh light, and hence in using them in a non-conventional way);

elaboration (the ability to build upon a simple idea or a few given facts).

Guilford does not suggest that these aspects of the human mind are sufficient for creativity. Potential alone is not enough: it is also necessary to consider personal temperament and motivation to create, subjects we shall discuss in detail in the next chapter.

How does the onlooker to this process decide whether the product is creative or not? What would most people agree had this elusive ingredient? A heart 'pacemaker'? The float glass process? A 'Sidewinder' air-to-air missile that homes in on the heat emitted by the engines of an enemy aircraft? Stockhausen's music? Electrostatic copying? An artificial kidney machine? 'Cats' eyes' in the road? Surrealism? Judgement will be made through the eyes of the beholder as well as those of the creator. For both it is an experience: for the creator it is the act of creation and the emotion accompanying it; for the observer it is the intellectual or aesthetic impact that the creation makes upon him. Parnes and Brunelle (1967) see it from the creator's viewpoint: 'Let us define creative behaviour as the production and use of ideas that are both new and valuable to the creator!' Stein (1963) takes the other view: '. . . a novel work that is accepted as tenable or useful or satisfying by a group at some point in time'.

Rogers (1959) speaks out clearly against any social evaluation, however: 'One man may be discovering a way of reducing pain, whereas another is devising a new and more subtle form of torture for political prisoners. Both these actions seem to me creative, even though their social worth is very different.' Criteria for the external judgement of creativity which do not include any measurement of social worth are provided by Golovin (1963): creative strength must be used to solve the problem; there must be a 'stride forward'; and there must be something unusual, remarkable and surprising in overcoming a special difficulty. Three very subjective and imprecise standards, but perhaps better than might be imagined, particularly if we solicit the opinions of those whose background and achievement classify them as experts. This suggestion comes from Doppelt (1964). Leaders in the field should be the best judges: their own level of achievement should give them an appreciation of the creative worth of an individual and his work. Although the public may make a different judgement, rejecting his work, perhaps, despite the experts' acclaim, his rating as a creator will be made by the latter.

But, Doppelt adds, judges are influenced by their own backgrounds as well as by the creator, and by other factors existing at the time. 'History is replete with instances of theories and practices rejected by the judges of one period and accepted as outstanding creative accomplishments at a different time.'

As part of the discussion in the external judgement of creativity we must consider the differences between scientific and artistic creation. An essential difference, it seems to me, lies in the reaction of the observer. Visual art, music and literature are judged in subjective, emotional, unsubstantial terms; scientific and technological achievement, on the other hand, is judged by its usefulness – immediate or eventual – in practical or intellectual terms. Whatever surprise, pleasure or satisfaction is stimulated by the elegance or appropriateness of a technical creation is incidental to its quality of usefulness. The emotional, intellectual or aesthetic response to creative art is its essence: it has no substance other than in the mind.

It is not argued here that the two are mutually exclusive. Architecture, for instance, is judged in terms of both beauty and usefulness. The elegance of the really great scientific and technological breakthroughs draws from the competent observer an admiration in which pleasure and intellectual approval are both present. Making light go around corners by means of fibre optics has just that effect; and there is something satisfyingly complete in Newton's Third Law of Motion: To every action there is an equal and opposite reaction.

Artists, musicians and writers rely on technological innovations for the expression and extension of their creative work. They are helpless without the tools of their craft: their paper, tools, cameras, paints, musical instruments, and increasingly, as they learn to use them, working aids such as typewriters, tape recorders and amplifiers. Indeed, creativity in technology will often stimulate creativity in the arts to use it. A new art form arose from the invention of the camera, and the electronics industry has provided musicians and the world of entertainment with the means of extending their activities to quite bizarre limits. Imagine a modern pop group without its vanload of amplifiers. Consider the complicated technology needed to create their powerful psychedelic effects. Think of computer-designed pictures and synthesized sound . . .

We began this chapter with a brief introduction to innovation, which is the prime concern of the book, and then paused to discuss creativity, an essential ingredient, from several different points of view. As a process, creativity was presented as something timeless and not wholly within our control, as a flash of inspiration producing form where no form existed a moment before. But one flash of inspiration did not produce Beethoven's *Choral Symphony*, Leonardo's *Mona Lisa* or Shakespeare's *Macbeth*. By general agreement each would be acclaimed as masterpieces of creative effort in detail and in the whole, but much more was needed to bring them to their finished state than just creativity – craftsmanship in applying the rules of the appropriate art form, analysis and judgement in achieving balance and effect, and sheer hard work in bringing all the bits together into one final composition. These works of art are as much examples of 'innovation' as the felt-tip pen described on page 7, on a different plane to be sure, but needing to go through essentially the same sequence from original concept to final product.

Technological innovation, like its artistic counterpart, is recognized by its end result. Any example we take is based on physical laws discovered and described by the scientist. It is not the part of technology and the engineer who serves it to discover these laws, but to create the artefacts that put them to practical use. Engineering, says the American Society for Engineering Education (1968), is the bridge between the world of science and the world of man. It is thus the application of the scientific discovery of the transistor to the radio and television industry; of the discovery of penicillin to the manufacture of antibiotic drugs; the process of polymerization to the manufacture of plastic utensils and textile fabrics; the laws of mathematics to the digital computer; the 'nitrogen cycle' to the artificial-fertilizer industry; the laws of magnetism to the tape recorder; distillation to the production of whisky and synthetic dyes; the Gas Laws to the refrigerator; the chemical properties of burnt limestone and clay to motorways, etc., etc.

Innovation is therefore a complex problem-solving sequence which in some way produces something novel yet tangible and complete. Its full cycle includes seven steps:

1. Perceiving some need or problem.
2. Gathering relevant facts and classifying the true nature of the problem.
3. Seeking new information and analysing the whole picture.
4. Proposing alternative ideas for a solution.
5. Evaluating and selecting a final solution for implementation.
6. Implementing the solution.
7. Verifying that the solution is satisfactory.

Creativity, while essential in step 4 to provide the novelty demanded by the word 'innovation', is by no means necessarily confined to this part of the sequence. Considerable ingenuity and downright creativity may be needed to achieve progress at any stage of the proceedings. Sometimes existing methods or materials will not be entirely satisfactory, and often human reactions to the change inherent in the innovation will call for a creative approach to overcoming these blockages.

Leaving the development of the wider aspects of the innovation sequence to later chapters, let us consider it here from the individual's point of view, his mental processes and the immediate external inputs and outputs. We have already admitted that we know little of the inner workings of the mind, but we can gain some understanding if we can imagine mechanisms and activities which somehow seem analogous to the processes going on inside us, and are intelligible to other people.

Guilford (1964) has led the way with a model, summarized in Fig. 2. The recycling nature of the sequence shown must be stressed from the start. The double-ended arrows signify repeated backtracking, checking, questioning and looping at all the stages. Though we may know what we want at the end we do not know how to achieve it when we start, and we will not know that we have arrived until we get there. The best we can hope for is to converge in a spiralling fashion on our target.

In Fig. 3 three areas of activity are suggested. The External Environment includes everything outside the person – all the physical, human and intellectual forces which have acted upon him and act upon him now, and have contributed to his store of information, skills, patterns of behaviour, values, opinions and prejudices, etc. Without trying to explain the how, where and what of this summation in any physiological way, we shall call this the unconscious part of the person (including in this term the

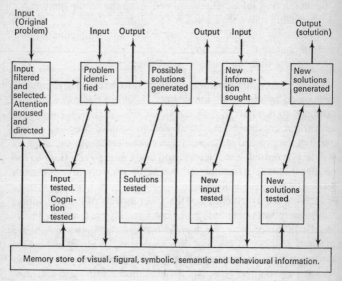

Fig. 2. Summary of Guilford's model of the innovation sequence.

preconscious system described on page 10). Here also take place certain involuntary mental activities such as memory formation and some problem-solving. The unconscious acts on the physical senses of the person, too, by modifying them to make him more or less aware of information received: acting in many ways like a highly selective filter. In between the physical senses and the unconscious is the conscious state of the person, where all his voluntary mental activity takes place, with input from both the external environment and the unconscious.

Suppose the person becomes aware of a problem in the external

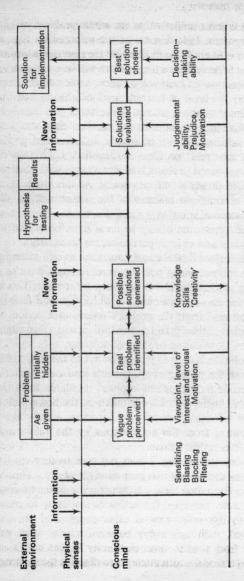

Fig. 3. Personal aspects of the innovation sequence.

environment. It is most unlikely that the whole problem will be immediately apparent. Indeed some of the information that is openly available is likely to be blocked by the filtering action of the senses. What is perceived as the problem will be examined by a conscious process which itself will be under some control from the unconscious: the level of interest, level of arousal and the 'frame of reference' adopted. Should the result of this examination conclude that there is more to the problem than was first thought, more information will be sought and admitted to the conscious until the 'real' problem is identified. Collection of more facts relevant to the problem is likely to ensue with possible solutions explored mentally and physically. At this stage some aspects of the unconscious makeup of the person will be all-important – his store of knowledge and skills, his motivation and interest, his willingness and ability to form hypotheses and to tolerate uncertainty and risk: in particular, his 'creativity'.

There is an important time element, too, when as well as acting as a storehouse and command post the unconscious can act as a problem-solving mechanism if it is left alone for a while. This is the mysterious incubation phenomenon, which acts at a time of deliberate withdrawal from the problem following a period of intense information-gathering and concentration, and which might lead to a sudden illumination or inspired solution.

However a solution is derived it must be put to the test, and it is judged against the problem requirements and other criteria imposed by outside factors or self-imposed standards from the unconscious. And lastly, a decision is taken on the best solution to implement, if more than one exist – a conscious activity again under some control from the unconscious by the values and intellectual abilities residing there.

The model suggested in Fig. 3 does not take us through the whole innovation cycle, only that part which is of a continuous personal nature. Even then there are excursions into the external environment. Later, however, the activities are likely to move much more into this outer area as other people and physical work is involved. Although highly personal mental work will still be needed from time to time, continuity for the individual will be lost, and a model which attempts to describe the sequence in terms of the mental activities of one person would become increasingly fragmented if pursued further. However, each personal contribution, in so far as it constitutes a problem-solving activity, will follow the basic sequence suggested in the model.

If the model is any good it should relate to real life. It does seem to, so far as it goes . . .

Imagine an electrical engineer given the problem of finding a way to make car-driving easier in fog. This is a real problem with no commercially marketed solution, so far as I know. Let us talk ourselves through an imaginary, but nonetheless humanly possible sequence of events from this point on. Our electrical engineer might immediately think of himself driving his car in thick fog with the accompanying feelings of frustration, tension and apprehension. The problem for him would centre on driving that car in greater comfort with reasonable certainty that he is not going to get hurt. Well, that is what the problem said, wasn't it? He has been paying attention and hasn't missed any words. And he is quite keen to have a go at solving it because he is a motorist and knows all the snags of driving in fog. But wait, he has heard the words and has reacted as a motorist. Hasn't he been a bit selective; hasn't he filtered the problem so that he has put only one possible meaning to it: that reflecting the point of view of a motorist? What if he hadn't driven a car? As a pedestrian would he have seen the problem in the same way? And did the problem really mean just making driving easier in fog? Didn't it also matter that he should know where he was going in addition to being able to drive easily and safely? Our motoring engineer must then widen his own perception and question the problem as given. Of course, he is told, the real problem is to find a way of driving in the fog which is easier for the driver, not hazardous for other road users and enables the driver to get to his destination. And don't forget, it hasn't to exceed £50, it must be light, compact and easily fitted, and it must be capable of operation by non-technical people . . .

Well, at least the problem is a bit clearer now. The motorist sits back for a moment while the electrical engineer takes over. Radar? Why not; but check cost and compactness, etc. . . . supposed to have been thought up by analogy with bats and their supersonic squeaks . . . Supersonics? Check that too! Blind people use the principle, don't they? Magnetic strips along the road? Would help in direction as well as distances from the kerb – like cats' eyes. Infra-red light? That sounds a distinct possibility ... But hang on; why the preoccupation with electrical means? Why not some simple mechanical system? And why can't we change the problem; get rid of steered vehicles and go back to tramcars? Because there is too much money tied up in motor cars and your job is to improve motor-car driving, not design a new transport system ... Some more constraints are appearing!

Let us interrupt here and imagine that the engineer finds out that all the leads he has thought up, and a host of others, have been tried without success, or at least without satisfying the requirements for cost, simplicity, etc. The electrical engineer and the whole man is now pretty well steeped in the problem: he has looked at it from several angles, he has tried unsuccessfully to fit a lot of possible solutions to it and he feels pretty frustrated. Confound it! It's time for a rest. Some time before, he had taken his family to the zoo. In the zoo there was an aquarium, and in the aquarium were some electric eels that could generate sufficient electrical energy to stun other fish. There was also a fish, *Gymnarchus niloticus*, that produced a weak electric field around it by which it sensed objects and other fish nearby, so enabling it to navigate and feed, for its eyesight was said to be poor. In the midst of his relaxation, and when occupied with something quite different, the idea suddenly comes: That fish! Why not an electric field around the car and some means of showing it pictorially. Why not!

Back at work again the engineer follows up the idea. With his own skill and knowledge and more information and suggestions from others he experiments, tests, modifies and develops until he has a working model; an electrode at the front of the car with a row of miniature sensors along each side, a power pack and a little screen inside which shows a couple of lines with bulges on them; the lines representing the road ahead for twenty-five yards and the bulges other cars and objects.

The engineer judges that this is the best solution he can offer. But does it work to the satisfaction of his boss and of those who will have to mass-produce it and sell it? Does it do all the things expected of it? Is some two-dimensional image of the road a few yards ahead sufficient to enable a driver to drive with comfort and to recognize where he is? How adequately does it solve the original problem?

Let us suppose there is sufficient promise to convince the firm to go ahead. The engineer's brainchild is now about to enter the outside world in earnest. Its future lies in others' hands. Too many resources, too much knowledge of special techniques, too many widespread activities are needed to design, erect and run an assembly line, to advertise, distribute and sell these gadgets for one man to hope to provide. The innovation cycle is far from complete, but the momentum to carry it through can no longer be provided by any one man. Even the final criteria against which its success will be judged will differ radically from those used by the engineer when testing his prototype. His desire for a technically elegant solution will be subordinated to customer appeal, sales and profit. The development of an innovation from this point on, however, will be left for discussion in later chapters.

2 The Personality Behind Innovation

In Chapter One we discussed the nature of creativity and innovation, seeing creativity as the quality of originality in something produced by the human mind, the mental ability to produce such novelty, or the actual activity of producing it. Innovation we introduced as the whole cycle of translating a piece of original thinking into something tangible. In this chapter we shall firstly consider the types of individuals whose personal makeup seems to be compatible with the special needs of creative and innovative expression, identifying a cluster of characteristics necessary for original thinking. Secondly we shall look at some of the theories which throw light on how such characteristics might have developed from a combination of inheritance and childhood experience. The next question, namely how specific learning and experience can develop creativity in later life, will be left until Chapter Four.

Before going any further, however, let us remember that, in addition to the creative person (the ideas man) and the innovator (the ideas man who translates his ideas into reality), there is a third person important in the process, the entrepreneur, who by his business ability takes an idea and develops it into a money-making proposition. He may not create ideas, but he follows the innovative cycle through, including the difficult and risky final phase of putting the product onto the market. Creator, innovator and entrepreneur, all three share an interest in novelty, in its creation, or its exploitation, or both, and it is useful to look at the whole picture in terms of the characteristics and behaviour of those who help to form it.

As we saw in Chapter One, creative strength is shown by the quality of a 'new synthesis of previously unconnected matrices of thought'. This means that the creative person is one who can bring together these matrices of thought in the most appropriate way. Creativity requires the destruction of something stable and accepted and its replacement by something new and untried (Abercrombie). It follows therefore that the creative person is also someone who can cast aside the constraints of hard fact and established principle, can tolerate the world of uncertainty and disorder he has entered into, and has the self-confidence to propose something new and defend it against the onslaught of criticism its novelty provokes. The creative act requires in addition a certain minimum of knowledge and information to provide the essential elements for the novel recombination: an Eskimo, however talented and skilled in his traditional way of life, cannot make an important breakthrough in nuclear engineering if he has never heard of the subject.

A wealth of literature exists on the creator and how to find him. Sometimes it doesn't differentiate between areas of creative expression; art or music, say, as distinct from science and technology. In the narrower area of technology, not much has been devoted to the creative scientist or engineer as separate breeds, and that which has provides considerable overlap and plenty of contradiction. We still have no infallible blueprint for such talented individuals nor are we likely to have if we accept that the expression of creativity is in part internal and personal and in part dependent on the external opportunities and pressures in an individual's environment. (The personal characteristics which have been attributed at some time or another to the creative person are so many and varied that creativity would seem to be an aptitude given to quite a large slice of the human race.) Considering creative scientists in particular, a list of twenty-six personality characteristics has been drawn up by Shapiro (1966) from a survey of 'virtually every study relating to creativity and personality'. Shapiro's creative scientist is outspoken, quick-thinking, self-centred, persuasive, impulsive, demanding, dedicated to research, intellectually curious, uninhibited, aggressive, intellectually adventurous, confident of his own ability, aesthetically inclined, intuitive, introverted and introspective, independent in judgement, flexible, emotionally unstable and sensitive, socially detached, radical and dominant; he has a sense of humour, a desire to achieve and broad theoretical interests, and he shows initiative.

McPherson (1967) gives a differently phrased list for creative engineers. They may vary in interests but are probably alike in being above average in certain kinds of intelligence, are dedicated to solving problems and pursue their goals aggressively though quietly. They are non-conformist in their ideas, 'often in conformist clothing to keep society off their backs'. Childlike and uninhibited in seeking ideas for testing, they are also extremely rigorous and scientific at other times. They have the guts to handle obstacles put in their way and show a general dissatisfaction with themselves and everything around them. These creative engineers, adds McPherson, find some autonomy and privacy for themselves, and, once found, they know how to use it. Management does not bother them too much and they have their own way of communicating effectively and getting the information they need.

This list is as much descriptive of a behaviour pattern as of basic personality, but its content does not do violence to the personality profile presented by Shapiro. No doubt there are differences in the strengths of some of the characteristics for scientists and engineers. Indeed, McPherson's list, more than Shapiro's, describes the active innovator rather than the idea-producing creator.

What sort of person is the technological entrepreneur, the third individual with a vital interest in creativity? Clearly he is at home at the frontier of scientific knowledge and yet is able to put his knowledge to use in producing some commercial 'hardware'. A very illuminating profile of the American entrepreneur is given in a study of the hundreds of technical companies which have grown up along Route 128, the motorway that circles Boston, with its cluster of advanced-technology laboratories centred on M.I.T. Roberts and Wainer (1968) of the Sloan School of Management of M.I.T. describe the typical founder of such a company. He has a fifty-fifty chance of coming from a home in which the father was in business himself, and his family background has encouraged a leaning towards entrepreneurship by the support and encouragement it has given him for personal achievement. He is about thirty-two when he starts his business and he has been engaged previously in development work rather than research. He is almost certain to have at least a bachelor degree: if he comes from a home with a higher occupational status, he will have a correspondingly higher level of education. But he will not be too highly qualified; if he is highly successful, he is more likely to possess an M.Sc. than a Ph.D. Roberts and Wainer say: 'The Ph.D.s as a group do not perform well as entrepreneurs. Their temperament, attitude and orientation are usually out of line with those needed for successful technical entrepreneurship.'

The high performers among these Route 128 entrepreneurs recognize the importance of business skills and marketing in their companies and are concerned about personnel matters. They have what McClelland (1961) calls a high need for achievement. This manifests itself in risk-taking, but at a level which, though presenting challenge, is potentially achievable, and in situations in which they can influence the outcome by their own efforts. They are not gamblers, willing to leave the outcome to chance or to others. Coupled with this moderate risk-taking is their decisiveness; hard work, especially in challenging original situations; acceptance of individual responsibility; a wish to know the result of their work; a concern for wealth as a measure of success; a forward-looking attitude; and organizational ability.

These technological entrepreneurs do not show a great urge for control over others. They do not play the power game or seek to command attention. Given the choice between an expert and a friend as a workmate they will choose the expert because their desire to excel at the job is greater than their wish to work with someone they like.

Creative, innovative and entrepreneurial aptitudes, then, seem to need many strengths in addition to special talents in a particular field. One way of representing such features is suggested by the Field Theory of Kurt Lewin (1951). According to this theory, a person is imagined to be subjected to forces acting upon him due to the attraction or repulsion of aspects of his environment which arouse tensions within him. These forces are 'vectorial' in nature, that is, they have specific strengths and directions, depending on the attraction or repulsion of the external goals and the strength of the inner tensions. If, for instance, the element in the environment is a problem requiring a novel solution, the tensions within the individual will be those associated with all the aspects of his personality which are involved in solving the problem – for example, his curiosity, confidence, intuition and dissatisfaction with the present situation. The resultant force influencing him to solve it will be proportional to the strengths of these tensions at any moment in time.

While these tensions can be aroused by the presence of a novel problem, they can also be stimulated by other factors in the environment unconnected with creativity (or entrepreneurial activity): curiosity can be associated with a desire to know as well as a wish to create, self-confidence can be roused and used to perform routine though difficult tasks. Each tension may therefore be considered to have a component which will relate to novel problems and a number of other components which will relate to quite different types of stimulation. We can imagine a person being subjected to pressure in various directions, each pull contributing something to his tendency to behave in a creative way. These creative components will add up to what might be called his 'creative resultant'; that is, his general disposition to think and act in a creative way. The situation is not static. All these tensions change with time and circumstance, and it is difficult to envisage a situation where they can be isolated and quantified. Nevertheless, they can be generally identified and seen to be positive or negative, aiding or restraining creative effort.

One imaginary 'tension field' is shown in Fig. 4. The strengths of these vectors have been chosen quite arbitrarily, as have the directions, except that those with components acting along the horizontal to the right are consistent with Shapiro's and McPherson's lists (though phrased differently) and those with components acting towards the left are some of the opposites. Factors such as 'athletic' or 'fair-haired' would be shown as vertical vectors since there is no apparent relationship between these and creative behaviour, and they therefore have no component in the horizontal, creative direction. All the vectors shown in Fig. 4 fall into one of three broad classifications:

1. Knowledge – specific and general information which acts as a store of building blocks for novel recombinations.
2. Intellectual abilities – mental skills which enable knowledge

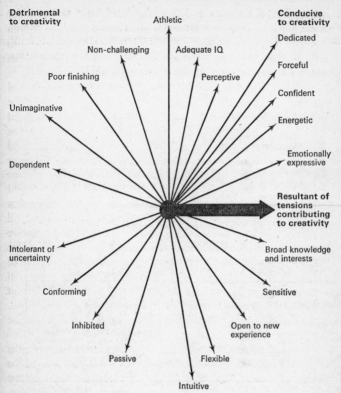

Fig. 4. Personality 'vectors'.

to be used effectively, including its recombination into new forms.

3. Temperament – emotional aspects of personality pertaining to level of energy, mood and activity which make a person more likely to use his skills and knowledge and to take the risk of entertaining and developing the novel ideas which may arise during their use.

Knowledge is related to the problems we have to solve, while temperament resides in the individual. Bridging the gap, so to speak, is skill, as shown in Fig. 5. For satisfactory performance, adequacy in all three areas is necessary. There is plenty of overlap between them. Knowledge and intellectual ability are obviously related, since the skill implied in the latter refers to the effective use of knowledge (like the craftsman's manual skill in using the

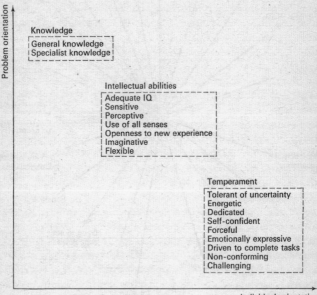

Fig. 5. Components of creative personality.

tools of his trade). Likewise, temperament and intellectual ability jointly govern a person's approach to his problems.

What is the specific nature of these characteristics and how do they contribute to creative and innovative behaviour?

Knowledge is a basic requirement for creativity. 'Nothing can be made of nothing,' says Reynolds, and the thought is developed by Guilford in his theory of the intellect. Without 'contents' (see page 15) there can be no 'products' because there is nothing to 'operate' on. Merely possessing knowledge however does not make anyone creative, nor does it mean that it will be used even when it is needed. Most of us fail to use much of the useful knowledge and experience we possess in solving a problem. Amongst the various areas of knowledge to which we have immediate access there are usually analogies for the picking, both in solutions and methods. Thermal insulation is analogous to electrical insulation; a mechanical valve in a pipe is analogous to an electrical switch in a wire; filtering light into different colours is analogous to the selection of different radio frequencies or separating the components of a chemical compound. The human body presents a vast array of analogies with electrical, mechanical and chemical systems. Communication theory has a foot in both psychology and electrical engineering camps and forms a growing conceptual link between the two; and so on. Using a multi-disciplinary team for tackling a problem is a recognized way of bringing different outlooks and bodies of knowledge to bear. We all have a multi-disciplinary system which can if we wish be applied to our problems instead of tunnelling into them in the one-tracked way dictated by our speciality.

Can too much knowledge inhibit creativity? It is sometimes suggested that inventions tend to be made by non-specialists in a particular field, implying that it is wise not to clutter our minds with too many facts. Yet this is surely not true. Knowledge itself cannot be a blockage; more likely it is an inability on the part of the expert to use what he knows by placing himself in a mental straitjacket and being unwilling to admit that there could be anything new in his area of expertise.

The creative person will readily admit that he is still learning. He may seem to be 'lucky' in his discoveries, but he is really *sensitive* to things around him and the materials – physical or conceptual – with which he works. His sensitivity is probably a combination of a conscious exploration and analysis of his environment and an intuitive response to low-level cues. The latter is the more important, for, being intuitive, it is not under conscious control and cannot be turned on and off at will. Rather it is an ever-present detection system which picks up significant 'signals', however weak, from the welter of 'noise'. Intellectually too it could be allied to the ability that creative people have to make

remote but highly appropriate associations. Most people neither
see nor appreciate the direction these signposts are indicating.

Allied to sensitivity is the creative person's *perception*. Fleming's
perception of the odd effect of a stray mould on his staphylococ-
cus bacteria culture ultimately gave us penicillin. Charles Goodyear's recognition of the effect of sulphur on rubber when the two
were brought together by chance resulted in the process of vul-
canization. The perception of significance in a chance event has
given us these and many other useful innovations, from Archi-
medes' Principle to polythene. For most of us perception is far

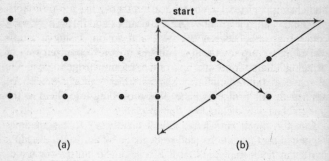

(a)   (b)

Fig. 6.

less acute, and more readily blunted by other factors. Maier
(1933) carried out a classical series of experiments on human
reasoning, some showing how past experience can come together
with present perception to solve a problem, and others demon-
strating how people often assume more limitations to a problem
than actually exist. Asked to draw four straight lines that pass
through all nine dots without lifting the pencil (Fig. 6a), many
people assume that the lines may not go outside the dots (Fig. 6b).
Similarly, when asked to form four equilateral triangles out of
six matches (Fig. 7), most people assume a two-dimensional approach and fail to solve the problem.

Most people have a built-in tendency to stabilize the world
around them. In an effort to cope with the enormous amount of
information bombarding us and the infinite number of problems,

great and small, which require immediate solution, we have evolved a mental system that tries to deal with them in ways which require less time and energy; that is, by habit and exclusion. When looking for novelty, this natural conservation of energy can be a positive hindrance. Our senses, in fact, have a remarkable breadth and versatility. The average human being can detect the taste of quinine at a concentration of about one half per million; see a candle flame 30 miles away on a clear dark night; hear a

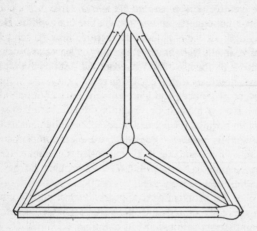

Fig. 7.

watch ticking at a distance of 20 feet; and smell musk at a concentration of only a few molecules per sniff. Yet we usually tackle a problem with a very small portion of the whole spectrum of that sensitivity. Of all the bits of information available about a problem, only a few become part of our actual experience and that part will be selected in a non-random way. We perceive some things, ignore others and positively reject still others. When reading these words it is unlikely that the reader will have been aware of the other things in plain view around them, still less the low-level background noises, smells and physical sensations which were present. Significantly, however, we are instantly aware of them when reminded of them. Isn't it the same with our perception of problems?

Information coming to us need not necessarily be at a conscious level to be useful. It has been suggested that medical diagnosis could be done by feeding in a stream of symptoms to a computer. However, the good diagnostician is sometimes at a loss to identify all the factors he takes into account. He is able to use signs which are somehow within his threshold but which elude description when an attempt is made to pinpoint them. He has a 'feeling' about them.

In *Invention, Discovery and Creativity*, A. D. Moore describes how the creative person *uses all his senses*. Give him a chunk of new plastic, he suggests, and notice what he does with it. He picks it up, gauges its weight, feels its texture, taps it, scratches it, squeezes it, smells it, bounces it: in short he learns as much about it as possible by the use of all his senses. He adds to this by asking questions: how was it made? will it resist heat? and so on. The creative person notices and learns much more about a situation than the average person by extending the range of experience open to him through the use of several sensing channels instead of one or two. His *openness to new information* is complemented by his flexibility in organizing it. His curiosity is childlike. He never loses the capacity to be surprised. Given a problem he may be the first to admit that he is puzzled, but his puzzlement will probably not be over the problem as it appears to most people but as he has already restructured and clarified it. His puzzlement may indeed be the first step toward its solution.

An essential part of his intellectual makeup is his *imagination*. Shaw wrote:

> Some people see things that are and ask why.
> I dream of things that never were and ask why not.
> (*Back to Methuselah*, Act I)

Using his imagination to create possibilities of what might be, he will play with ideas, let his mind wander, visualize ideal solutions and look for stepping stones back to reality. This daydreaming is productive, for it enables him to explore possibilities which may lead him to question facts of life. He puts into practice the dictum of science-fiction writer Arthur Clarke, that the only way of finding the limits of the possible is by going beyond them into the impossible.

Most people find it easier to talk about things they know than about things they don't know. Creative people willingly acknowledge their areas of ignorance, not because they feel inadequate or ashamed but because that is where their interest lies. A successful manager of Research and Development in the United States steel industry uses this notion in staff selection. He says he would look for people who are drawn instinctively to the unknown rather than the known when they are being interviewed. The man who shows an interest in science fiction or who can dwell happily on the state of our ignorance as much as on our knowledge is the man he would pick for creative engineering.

A *flexible* mind is essential to the creative thinker if he is to remain free and unblocked by imagined or habitual constraints, yet be capable of high discrimination and concentration when the complexity of the problem demands it. If he is to wed logical reasoning to feeling, intuition and sensitivity, then the creative person has to possess and tolerate a wide range of behaviour within himself, and to integrate it to maintain a balance in his mental activity. 'He makes guesses, and he applies rigorous logic to test out his guesses. He is capable of engaging in both spontaneous and systematic communication. He is adept at thinking in different directions as well as in a single direction. He is independent, but he is also dependable' (Hitt, 1965).

Our paragon of creative virtue is a clear-sighted individual. To be sure, he can drift off into orbit with his flights of fancy, but within his area of work he also has a high power of resolution and can clarify and order his thinking.

There is much analytical and convergent thinking in the preparatory phase of creative problem-solving. Kuhn (1963) describes the interplay between this divergent and convergent thinking of the creative scientist as the 'essential tension' which helps to give him his special talent, adding '. . . very often [he] must simultaneously display the characteristics of the traditionalist and of the iconoclast'. He must be firmly rooted in contemporary knowledge, yet be able to break out of it.

Can too much knowledge inhibit creativity? we asked earlier, and answered with the suggestion that it was not knowledge itself that caused the blockage but its effect on the flexibility of our thinking. Any problem that we meet in our area of specialist experience triggers off a train of thought and memories of solutions which make it difficult to think independently of them. Indeed a manifestation of our skill is the smooth, effective flow of reactions to some stimulus which requires no close conscious control. The skill of hitting a golf ball right may require much practice, but when mastered is a sequence of physical operations which is positively harmed by self-conscious control. Any 'adjustment' to this skill requires an unlearning and a period of relearning of something slightly different.

Clearly any economy we can achieve by learning chunks of knowledge and patterns of behaviour is important in dealing with the complexity of life. But it is a real hindrance to the creation of new possibilities unless we have learned the higher skill of applying what we know while preventing it from interfering with our mental flexibility. Habit, 'set' and expectation not only dim our perception, they also have a tramline effect on thought processes. The similarity of a problem to ones we have met before, the effect of the same environment and the success of the solutions we have used, all conspire to make us follow a well-trodden path from problem to solution without checking that the problem is really the same or the solution is really appropriate. Try saying the following words one after another:

MACINTOSH
MACTAVISH
MACBETH
MACDOUGAL
MACHENERY
MACHINE

The mental 'set' produced by the recital of the clans often results in the last name being pronounced wrongly. If this happens with simple problems, how much more is it likely to happen in more complex situations! We need to check periodically to make sure that rigidity is not setting in, and at the same time decide what shall be delegated to habit and well-tried solutions. We cannot treat every situation as a problem for ingenuity.

Disorder is a necessary part of the creative sequence if novelty is to grow out of harmony, and uncertainty in intellectual and personal terms go with it. An engineer trying to find some radically new method of transport is working in a technical wilderness: within himself he is not sure where he is going. All he knows is that he is adrift with a strong chance of failure. If he is truly creative he can tolerate this uncertainty and work through the disorder between the old level of achievement and a higher one that he is creating. He can hold back from accepting the first solution that offers itself if it does not give a proper sense of rightness and elegance. He can explore in many directions and in many levels; he can stop and go back to square one and start again; he can use different methods of approach; and can discard old ones as easily as he can adopt new ones. He is a self-starter, but he can stop and take a rest. He can immerse himself in his problem, live with it, live for it, but withdraw from it when he is making no headway. He knows the value of relaxation, of defocusing and of catching things out of the corner of the mind's eye.

There is a large slice of self-sufficiency in the makeup of the successful creator. He relies on his own *energy* as well as his own ability: he does his own thing and is willing to work hard at it. Edison is reported to have worked for five days and nights at one time during the development of his phonograph, and regularly took no more than four or five hours' sleep while working on his inventions. Innovators have a high maternal feeling for their brainchildren, even though they may themselves have no preconceived idea of their usefulness. Rutherford, who split the atom, could see no practical use for this achievement. Michael Faraday, when asked what use the dynamo which he had invented would be, could only reply, 'What use is a baby?'

Such *dedication* is an essential factor in the makeup of the successful innovator. Whittle's obsession with his concept of the jet engine made him the laughing stock of his R.A.F. station. King Camp Gillette spent nine years developing and marketing his safety razor. Charles Goodyear dedicated himself, his wealth, his family life and many years of hard research and experimentation into perfecting his method for vulcanizing rubber. Isambard Kingdom Brunel, the Victorian engineer who built the Great

Western Railway from Paddington station to Bristol – and then coolly extended the service to New York by building the first economic Atlantic liner – was always in the forefront with technological innovations. Some were huge successes, like his railway and his bridges; some were resounding failures! His monster ship the *Great Eastern* was six times bigger than any ship then afloat, was a nightmare to build and when launched was a commercial flop. His atmospheric railway was basically sound, working on the principle of a continuous vacuum maintained in a tube which drew the train along via a 'shoe' entering into the tube through a leather flap. Unfortunately rats ate the leather and ruined the whole system. To Brunel, engineering innovation was all-important and he spent his life in pursuit of the biggest and best in technology. He died while the *Great Eastern* was being fitted out, continuing to supervise the work from his sick-bed after suffering a stroke on top of a kidney disease. Dedication shows itself in the high standard of performance that creative people demand of themselves in their chosen field. Persistence of this kind is an all-important factor in the behaviour of highly creative people (see Maddi, 1965).

Self-confidence is also important. A person must have faith in his own ability in order to face an open-ended problem for which there is no ready-made solution. He has to make a creative step forward if he is to solve it, with only the aid of his own skills and knowledge. Allied to his faith must be optimism. He can solve the problem, and he will! Small increments in achievement give him sufficient encouragement. Near misses, instead of representing failures, serve as incentives to do better next time. Accepting the risk of failure is natural: he of all people knows how seldom success will come his way, for inevitably most of his novel ideas are unworkable.

The innovator must not only be confident in himself to develop his idea but must also *force it onto others*. This will not be achieved by forbearance and humility but by a decidedly single-minded assertiveness, a desire to explain the idea to anyone who will listen and a determination to gain support for it. To know success, then, he must know how to influence other people and how to use them. He may be sensitive to their needs, not necessarily out of sympathy for them, but to gain commitment to his cause. Influence will be by logical argument more than emotional appeal for the scientist, however, for he will avoid too personal an approach, preferring to deal with things or abstractions rather than people. When Barnes Wallis was rebuffed by the Air Council over his idea for an earthquake bomb during the war he wrote a treatise on his bomb and circulated it to seventy people of influence in politics, science and the Services. He was reprimanded by the security people, got an introduction to Henry Tizard, who was scientific adviser to the Ministry of Aircraft Production – and the support he needed.

Though a creative person is quick to foster and defend his work, he is less likely to be concerned over opinions about himself. He has a certain personal detachment which insulates him. This is not to say that he is unfeeling or bottles up his emotions. On the contrary, he is likely to react strongly, particularly when his work is under attack, and *give vent to his feelings* forcibly. Likewise, his delight with fresh discovery or achievement can be open and expressive. Charles Vernon Boys was a scientist who, among other things, measured the gravitational constant so accurately that its value was unchallenged for fifty years. Moore (1969) recounts how, when Boys made a discovery, he let everyone know about it: 'He would come out of his laboratory whooping and yelling and leaping over tables and chairs.'

There seems to be in most of us a drive to complete something once started. Rickers-Ovsiankena (1937), for instance, found that over 70 per cent of normal people returned to an interrupted task at the first opportunity to finish it, and Lewin (1935) observed that most people tested recalled more of a problem that was interrupted than those that were completed. This effect was greater for more difficult tasks and with people who were interrupted just before completion. Creative people have this *drive to complete tasks* and feel a special tension when there is a lack of completeness of 'closure' in what they see. A sense of dissonance caused by the problem itself makes them uncomfortable until they have solved it. Bertrand Russell, quoted by Hutchinson (1949), mentions the feeling: 'In all the creative work that I have done, what has come first is a problem, a puzzle involving discomfort. Then comes concentrated voluntary application entailing great effort. After this a period without conscious thought, and finally a solution . . .' It may be that for such people it is a strong appreciation of pattern in intellectual or physical form which gives them a drive to seek solutions which are more complete in their integration of the problem field – good solutions rewarding them with that pleasant Aha! feeling at the moment of perception. Creative people can use this feeling as a signal that they have achieved 'something', for often, as mentioned in Chapter One, it is felt before there is time to organize thought to express its meaning.

They can also pursue creativity just for the gratification it gives them. Maddi (1965) indeed suggests that their high need for novelty is not for its own sake, but for the particular pleasure that accompanies it. Certainly they show delight in achievement, especially when they produce something that is both sound and aesthetically pleasing. Speaking of scientists, engineers and architects in particular, MacKinnon (1961) says, 'For the truly creative person it is not sufficient that the problem be solved; there is the further demand that the solution be elegant!'

Non-conformity in the creative person is to be expected, at least in his work, and he may do and say things that suit his way of working even if it outrages the establishment. His behaviour may indeed be decidedly abnormal; but not necessarily so. Vernon (1970) comments: 'Many men of genius in the past have shown psychotic or severe neurotic tendencies, and it is difficult to believe that they could have produced as they did had they been more normal. Many others have been eccentrics, rebels or emotionally unstable, while still others have lived full and very ordinary lives, though characterized by extreme devotion to their artistic or scientific work.' Of things scientific Faraday was a daring and original thinker, yet in all other ways he was conventional in his behaviour. Lord Kelvin combined eminence in pure science and technical invention. Outside his science he was described as a typically respectable and business-like Scot.

Edwin Land (1959), inventor of the Polaroid camera, tells how he repeated Newton's original experiments of passing a narrow beam of sunlight through a prism to produce the full visible spectrum on a screen. Then, just like Newton, he produced single colours from the spectrum by blocking off the rest with a slotted board. Next he mixed two pure, but different colours, and, as expected, obtained the compound of the two. Repeated with two tones of yellow from opposite ends of the yellow band, the resultant mixture was yellow. All very obvious. Then he did something different. He took two almost identical, black and white photographs of a group of coloured objects, the only difference being that each was taken through a different filter, one passing long wavelengths (for example, red) and the other passing short wavelengths (say, green). The negatives, let us repeat, were black and white, not colour. When he placed this pair of transparencies in front of two yellow beams of only slightly differing wavelengths the resulting image on the screen contained all the colours of the original objects. In this situation, the rays were clearly not making all these colours, but were in some way giving information to the eye by which it assigned appropriate colours to the objects on the screen. Newton's experiments and conclusions about colour were not wrong, but his work was all concerned with spots of light, not with colour vision under natural conditions. Land 'twisted' the obviousness of Newton's conclusions to see if the particular applied in general; and it did not.

With the benefit of hindsight, of course, it is easy to see later how blind the opponents of innovations have been. But it takes a rare combination of clear thinking, imagination and courage to see through all the incontrovertible features, to be undaunted by the intellectual respectability that surround them and to pick out the significant flaws in the picture.

Having discussed the special cluster of factors which are associated with creative and innovative personalities, let us consider the more general question of how personality is developed: how, simply, we become what we are. Allport (1961) defines personality as 'the dynamic organization within the individual of those psychophysical systems that determine his characteristic behaviour and thought', a definition which includes all the factors which manifest themselves in some sort of activity – abilities, motives, attitudes, values, interests and typical modes of adjustment to circumstances, etc. How do all these traits develop? Are they inherited, formed by the environment in which we live or a combination of both? The answer is of course the latter. Our individual inheritance predisposes us to develop a certain personality profile, but whether we actually develop to the peaks of this profile depends upon our home experiences and the socializing effects of our culture. It is probably fruitless even to speculate on what separately came from the nature and nurture provided by the famous Stephenson and Brunel fathers to their equally famous sons or how the musical achievements of Bach and Strauss were repeated in the next generation.

There are many theories on the development of personality. We will mention three here, concentrating on what they say about the development of the creative and innovative personalities.

The first is that of Piaget, whose views on intelligence as an adaptation to the environment were briefly mentioned in Chapter One. Piaget describes the development of intelligence through childhood as a number of major identifiable stages. Flavell (1963) describes four main stages, each with smaller divisions, which every person must pass through in sequence, though the transition is blurred and only approximately linked to the particular age limits. For the first two years of life, the child develops from a state of utter dependency and unperceiving self-centredness to a level where he has a rudimentary language, a host of means–end actions and a perception of himself as something different from the rest of the world. During the next five years there is an essential lawlessness about his world – anything is possible because nothing is subject to lawful constraints. But then his world stabilizes. He learns the rules of living and the laws of nature – the conservation of weight and shape and quantity – and he obeys and applies them rigidly. He becomes, in Flavell's words, 'a sober and book-keeperish organizer of the real and a distruster of the subtle, the elusive and the hypothetical'. Lastly, by eleven or thereabouts, he breaks through this concrete ordering of things and begins to manipulate hypotheses and possibilities in his mind. He deduces and imagines. He can free himself from limitations and yet return to test his flights of fancy against reality. He combines his earlier mental liberty with his later respect for the rules. Or, as Flavell puts it, 'He can soar; but . . . it is a controlled and planned soaring, solidly grounded in a bedrock of careful analysis and painstaking accommodation to detail.' Not everybody reaches the final stage of development and among those who do there is a considerable variation in the level achieved. And in the same person there may not be the same level of attainment in all tasks: at times he may regress to earlier modes of thinking.

Piaget's four stages offer some interesting points concerning creative thinking. The complete unlawfulness of the second stage is reminiscent of the state of mind advocated for the generation of fresh ideas: regression of this sort would seem to be a useful strategy. The fourth and final stage, where the person can stand with his head in the clouds and his feet on the ground, is more in keeping with the state of mind referred to by Kuhn (page 39) in describing the interplay between divergent and convergent thinking within the mature creative scientist. Proper balance between the two, however, is the essential factor.

A theory dealing with the development of motivation of the normal person through a five-level hierarchy of needs is given by Maslow (1954, 1959). In ascending order these needs are:

Physiological needs (hunger, thirst, sex)
Safety needs (security, shelter, freedom from attack)
Belonging and love needs (affection, friendship, belonging-to a group)
Esteem needs (self-respect, self-confidence, prestige)
Need for self-actualization (self-fulfilment, creativity, self-expression)

According to Maslow, these needs appear in the order given during the normal development of the individual, and earlier needs have to be satisfied before much energy is available for later ones. Many people will never manage to satisfy the lower needs to enable them to reach the self-actualization level. But those who do may show a combination of childlike innocence of perception and spontaneity of expression and practical wisdom. The 'self-actualizing' person is a healthy, highly evolved and mature individual, whose fundamental needs are satisfied to the extent that they no longer dominate his behaviour. He may show a creative

approach to any or all of his activities. This self-actualizing creativity is an expression of his personality and is not the same as
'special-talent creativity'. Maslow is careful to make this point.

In addition to his childlike naïvety, the self-actualizing person
has what Rogers (1959) calls an 'openness to experience'; he can
learn from anybody with something to teach; he accepts himself
as he is and behaves in a natural, non-defensive way. He has an
independent turn of mind and does not find the unknown too
frightening. An ability to integrate seeming opposites is shown in
his healthy selfishness, his maturity and his childlike perception,
and his ability to make play out of work.

The psychoanalytic theory of personality development is the
third theory which we shall examine briefly. Freud believed that
personality has a three-part structure: the 'id', where reside
instinctive drives demanding instant satisfaction without regard
to reality or morality, energy provided for these motives being
called 'libido'; the 'ego', which deals more realistically with the
world through learned ways of thinking and behaving; and the
'superego' which acts as a conscience, restraining both id and ego
and maintaining ideals and standards learned in childhood. Since
both the ego and superego block the libido's natural outlets it
may be displaced into more acceptable behaviour, but, because
of the conflict aroused, the person may experience anxiety which
he will try to reduce by defence mechanisms such as projection,
in which he disguises a motive he finds unacceptable in himself by
ascribing it to somebody else; repression, a convenient 'forget-
ting'; displacement, in which he transfers attention from one
object or goal to another to disguise his anxiety about the original
one; rationalization, in which he claims an acceptable motive for
his behaviour to hide the unacceptable one that his behaviour
actually expresses; and fantasy, in which he gratifies frustrated
motives in his imagination. Speaking of artists in particular,
Freud (1920) describes the process this way. 'He is impelled by
too powerful instinctive needs. He wants to achieve honour,
power, riches, fame and the love of women. But he lacks the
means of achieving these satisfactions. So like any other unsatis-
fied person, he turns away from reality and transfers all his interests, his libido, too, to the elaboration of his imaginary wishes . . .

Apparently their constitutions are strongly endowed with an ability to sublimize and to shift the suppression determining their conflicts. The artist finds the way back to reality in this way.'

Freud held that a person passes through a number of stages in childhood, each associated with a different part of the body: the oral stage, anal stage, phallic stage and genital stage. During each stage he gets most satisfaction from that part of his body, but over- or under-gratification may result in a fixation of the feelings and behaviour characterizing that stage. Thus the compulsive working of the creative scientist could be associated with the anal stage, the result of excessive toilet training which arouses anxiety leading to special satisfaction in control of the bowels and thence to self-control and compulsiveness.

Though Freud's description of the origins of individual behaviour may be questioned by many, there is less doubt that the special qualities shown by creative people owe something to childhood experiences and the inner tensions they generate – tensions which if resolved might well rob them of an essential ingredient of their creativity.

Though different in their approach and scope these three theories have a common assumption that personality develops in childhood through a series of fixed stages, giving us at maturity a relatively stable pattern of intellectual behaviour and motivation. Piaget's and Maslow's theories are more applicable to 'normal' creative expression than to the work of genius, while the insights of Freud touch on the latter much more rare occurrence. None claims that personality ever reaches a rigid unalterable form. We shall return to this subject in Chapter Four when we discuss some of the ways in which at least the peripheral parts of our intellectual and temperamental makeup can be developed.

3 Identifying the Problem

'There has always been a problem first. I have never had a novel idea in my life. My achievements have been solutions to problems . . . things have never come in a flash: they come only as a result of months, even years, of very heavy work.' These are the views of Barnes Wallis. His words echo those of Bertrand Russell, whom we quoted in Chapter Two (page 43): 'In all creative work that I have done, what has come first is a problem . . .'

Sometimes we can be creative without the stimulus of an immediate problem. Novel ideas do arise spontaneously in some people's minds without a history of search and effort to find a solution. Yet when random thought results in a notion which rises unbidden in the mind but which is recognized instantly as something new and satisfying, this subjective assessment itself must be against some criterion, some problem however vaguely conceived, which is henceforth solved. Could it be that the multitude of problems that we are faced with and fail to solve day after day sink down into the unconscious, and those flashes of unexpected revelation are merely the result of unbidden but enduring incubation?

Whether or not all creativity is problem-solving, seeking out the right problem to solve is an essential prelude to profitable technological innovation. And problem recognition must start with a search for discrepancies between what is and what might be and end with a clear statement of this mismatch in simple, unambiguous terms. The gap in the technological jigsaw must be found and, equally important, the shape and pattern of the piece we are seeking must be described clearly and accurately.

Speaking on 'Originality' in the United States, the psychologist Norman H. Mackworth (1965) went so far as to declare that problem-finding is more important than problem-solving. It is a much more complex process, he suggested, and the bottleneck in scientific progress is the rate at which problems can be identified, not the rate at which they can be solved. 'Scientific progress is no longer determined by the number of people who are good at solving problems because already the supreme problem-solvers of our day are machines.'

Now, nearly a decade later, we have machines taking the drudgery out of repetitive manual and mental work, solving mathematical problems at superhuman speeds, and acting more and more as if they had human intelligence. But they cannot yet produce solutions which are non-predictable from the evidence available at the start – they cannot display free imagination. Nor can they solve problems which involve factors for which there are as yet no valid dimensions, though they may be open to personal and subjective assessment: problems involving human values, aesthetics, morals and beliefs. Until the machine can work in all the dimensions man's mind is capable of appreciating, and can demonstrate unpredictable 'inspiration' in the fit and blend of its solutions, it cannot supplant man. But it can be a very useful partner.

So, however much of the problem-solving sequence we can delegate to the machine, we must still find our problem in the first place, and describe it with precision in the most suitable mode – verbally, pictorially or mathematically – for on this will depend the shape of the final solution.

The first task then is to clarify what the real problem is. Is it a deviation from a situation that is generally satisfactory – as when a car engine suddenly runs hot but only needs water to top up the radiator, or a new thermostat, to put things right? Or is it an exception from the general rule – the car runs hot only after a couple of hours' running? Or a need for improvement – the car springing is just not good enough for the wife and family? Or a need for optimization – the driver's wish to have the best compromise between acceleration ability and petrol consumption? Perhaps it is none of these, but is concerned with the future – what is going to succeed the internal combustion engine as a means of powering personal transport?

Wherever we think the problem is, it is always wise to augment our thinking by putting some order and substance into the diagnosis, writing things down, drawing a diagram, or somehow feeling our way into the problem. An engineer faced with a problem will soon have pencil and paper out and be explaining the situation with the aid of a sketch, or, given something to touch and manipulate, he will turn it this way and that, pushing it, prodding it and generally getting the feel of it. In these ways the problem is made more familiar, concrete and personal.

One of the most powerful methods, and the simplest, for getting at the real problem is to gather all the facts and symptoms together and to subject the whole mess to Critical Examination, which asks the questions:

What (is at present achieved/is proposed/is needed)? Why?
How?   Why?
When?   Why?
Where?   Why?
Who?   Why?

In following through such a sequence of questioning we break the problem down into recognizable components which increase understanding and help to restate the problem with more precision. When we have sifted out all that is irrelevant and inaccurate we must still be careful. The plainest of problems may, on closer examination, turn out to have many facets. Take a simple example: an unsatisfactory door catch on a domestic cooker.

Problem: design an efficient door catch for the cooker.
Why? To keep the door closed.
Why? To keep the heat in and ensure even cooking.
Why? To cook the food.
Why? To make it digestible and appetizing.
Why? To enable people to eat a wider variety of food than exists in a digestible uncooked form.
And so on . . .

If we carried on, we could soon be spelling out the problems of world food shortage, religious taboos on certain food, the eating habits of civilized man, or whatever. The point is that by asking the question 'Why?' we can expand the original problem out of all recognition. What was a simple mechanical engineering problem becomes one of heat conservation or distribution, of nutrition or social habit – each requiring a very different approach and body of knowledge to solve it. And the route chosen in this hierarchy of problems is not the only one that could have been followed. We could have chosen to follow the continuing sale of cookers, or the interests of the producers of foods requiring cooking. Only one thing is certain: the further we step away from the problem, the more we see it in a wider system and the better the chance we have of finding a more comprehensive solution. If we had chosen to accept it as first presented, it is likely that we would have got a better catch for the oven. By standing back we got the beginning of a list of more fundamental problems, any of whose solutions could conceivably have swept aside the need to solve the original one.

This is not the only way of twisting the problem around to gain a new perspective. Osborn (1953) gives a whole checklist for enabling us to expand our view in order to see the problem in a different way:

Adapt?
Modify?
Magnify?
Minify?
Substitute?
Rearrange?
Reverse?
Combine?

Von Fange (1959) goes further, but on a narrower front:

What about shape, size?
What if reversed, inside out, upside down?
What else can it do?
What can be left out?
What if carried to extremes?
What if symmetrical? Asymmetrical?
Can it be safer?
Can it be cheaper?
Slide instead of rotate?
Can it move? Can it be stationary?

The question 'What if carried to extremes?' forms the basis of the Hazard and Operability Studies used in the design of chemical process plants to examine the effects of mistakes in operation, accidents or breakdowns of components. Starting with a basic description of the process, including what materials are put in, what is done to them and under what conditions, deviations from the normal are considered. For example, at some part of the sequence it could be postulated: 'More of chemical A is present than there is supposed to be.' The causes of this abnormal state of affairs would then be sought, followed by all possible effects, both local and remote, to give a clear picture of conditions over the whole plant in this situation. By following the examination through in a systematic way the implications of all deviations can be considered, and means of avoiding or containing undesirable effects incorporated into the plant design.

The analytical approach of critical examination thus helps strip away irrelevancies and false symptoms and present the problem in its essence. It may also be necessary to diverge and look all round the problem again in an open-ended way to discover an appropriate opening leading to a practical solution. In describing the 'Synectics' method of problem-solving (see page 84) Gordon uses the apt phrases 'Making the strange familiar', which implies stripping away all uncertainty and stating the problem in unequivocal terms, and 'Making the familiar strange', which implies looking at the problem in a new way as a stimulus for a novel solution.

When the problem has been boiled down to its essence it may be in such a general form that it can be identified by analogy in a number of quite unconnected areas, sometimes even with ready-made solutions which might provide ideas for solving the original problem. Let us take the problem of developing a new paint and concentrate on the concept of paint in a freewheeling sort of way:

What is paint? It is a decorative and protective covering.
Protective covering? Gives protection; provides a skin; is an
     interface, a boundary layer . . .
Boundary layer? Where else do we find boundary layers?

Biology? The bark of a tree is a boundary layer. It is self-healing . . .

The surface of a leaf is part of the photosynthesis mechanism . . .

Physiology? Skin is also a boundary layer. Damaged physically it bleeds and clots, then forms scar tissue. It is permeable and helps in the regulation of body temperature. It is pliable and soft yet maintains its shape . . .

Physics? Electric charges act at surfaces to attract and repel . . .

Chemistry? Membranes are boundary layers but are permeable – let things pass in one direction and not in another . . .

Atmospherics? Layers in the stratosphere have different densities . . .

Crime? Boundary layer between cops and robbers – informers, who help identify harmful elements in society . . .

None of these questions and answers solve the original problem, but they do give several new approaches from which solutions might possibly be developed. For instance:

1. Could a paint be made self-healing?
2. Could a paint be developed to play a part in a wider process such as the absorption and release of moisture to maintain a relatively fixed level of humidity in a room?
3. Could a paint be charged electrically to repel dirt, or to combat corrosion of the material it was covering?
4. Could a paint be made to be self-layering?
5. Could a paint be made to give an indication of incipient damage or deterioration?

Problems once identified can then be categorized. This helps us to decide the most appropriate way for tackling them: whether a novel solution is needed or whether one taken from our stock of ready-made answers will be adequate. There appear to be three broad types of problem: problems of deviation; problems of development; problems of speculation. All the approaches which have been described already are applicable to problems in general, but there are additional techniques which can be used in more specific ways.

The Problem as a Deviation

Two American consultants, C. H. Kepner and B. B. Tregoe (1965), have developed a rigorous method for problem analysis where the problem is a deviation from some on-going standard and is of sufficient magnitude to warrant corrective action. The problem must have had a cause which can be described specifically before a decision can be made on the best solution to it. Seven basic steps in problem analysis are given:

1. An expected standard of performance, together with acceptable variations from this standard, is defined for comparison with actual performance.
2. The problem is considered as a deviation from the standard of performance outside the variations allowed.
3. This deviation is described precisely in terms of identity, location, time and extent; what it includes and does not include.
4. That which has been affected by the cause and that which has not been affected is analysed to distinguish the factors which differentiate one from the other.
5. The cause of the problem is specified in terms only of the changes which have been found relevant to the problem.
6. Propositions consistent with the facts as to the possible cause are stated, with a minimum of assumptions.
7. The problem to be tackled is the one which is most consistent with the facts.

Another American method similar to the Kepner–Tregoe in approach is the Zero Defects method. The starting point is a deviation from a standard which is identified and classified as a defect or error. Such a defect is then traced to all possible causes in the areas of men, machines or materials. Intended as a forward-looking discipline, the goal of Zero Defects is to get a job done correctly from the start by identifying and removing causes of errors and mistakes. Clearly it has value for problem diagnosis, whether the problem is embedded in an existing system or is anticipated in the design stage of a new product or process. Both the Kepner–Tregoe and the Zero Defects methods have much in common with Critical Examination, to which we have already referred. All three methods seek to isolate and clarify problems within a mass of irrelevant information: they provide a means of separating the signal from the noise.

The Problem as a Development

In a sense this is the same as a deviation problem, except that instead of looking for the harmful deviation from normal so as to bring the system back to its original healthy state, this approach speculates on a change which can be imposed on the system to make it better than it was. Perhaps the simplest question to be asked in seeking a starting point for development is, Can what we have be simplified? Real advance is often achieved by taking away the frills, eliminating redundancy, combining functions, substituting other materials, changing layouts and sequences, and so on. Allen H. Mogenson (1965) has developed a formal Work Simplification Method which includes a checklist approach to isolating possible areas for improvement:

1. Select the area for improvement – where are the bottlenecks, the delays and the waste?
2. Collect the facts and present them in an orderly way by process, procedure or activity charting, sketching components, etc.
3. Challenge all details using the technique of questioning What? Why? When? How? Where? Who?
4. From the possibilities emerging from this analysis, develop simpler and more effective methods or products.

In the same vein, but not focusing specifically on simplification, is Attribute Listing. The method again follows a set sequence:

1. Describe each component of the object or product in factual, physical terms – its shape, dimensions and material.
2. Describe the function of each component – its purpose and the reason for its choice.
3. Consider each attribute of every component in turn, changing it in all conceivable ways and relating the changes to the rest of

the equipment, with a view to improving its function or form, or reducing its cost.

As a simple example, let us take an ordinary drinking cup. We could describe it as follows:

Cup – $\frac{1}{4}$ pint capacity

Component	Attribute	Function
Container	3½ in. high, 2½ in. diameter, vertical, closed at lower end	Contain a given amount of liquid
	Approximately cylindrical	Prevent too easy slopping over. Easy to drink from. Stable when standing
	Rigid	Permanency
	China or earthenware	Robustness. Insulation for hot liquids. Lightness
	Decorated	Pleasant to look at
	Glazed	Protection for decoration. Easy to clean. Non-toxic
Handle	Shaped to fit fingers	Ease of holding container when hot. Convention

Without being too exhaustive, it is easy to see that the process opens up several areas for further questioning. Is the size really the one that most people desire? Can a cup be made more robust by changing its shape or material? Can its heat-conducting properties be decreased? Or its radiating properties increased to cool down hot liquids more quickly? Do we really need a handle? What about simplicity and cheapness as alternatives to robustness and aesthetic appeal? Many of these questions have been answered by the arrival of unbreakable cups, throw-away paper cups, insulated beakers and so on, each showing some change in one or other of the attributes of the traditional cup.

Attribute Listing is equally applicable to a chemical or physical product – providing a means of displaying its composition, physical state and present uses, and acting as a starting point for developing further uses for its properties.

Concentrating on the cost of each function in the Attribute Listing method gives us the novel contribution of Value Analysis.

By examining the cost of providing each component against the function it performs, we can question its worth to the purpose of the whole object and identify areas for simplification, modification or elimination. The value of concentrating on the ratio $\frac{\text{function}}{\text{cost}}$ is shown by some illuminating figures taken from exercises in Value Analysis:

45 per cent of the total cost of a canteen oven went to the function 'Look good'.

In a chemical process, 18 per cent of the cost went into providing access to equipment.

11 per cent of the total cost of a building went into achieving a layout which was neither needed nor requested.

20 per cent of the cost of a pumping plant went into providing extra but unquantified reliability – and a further 19 per cent was added 'to make quite sure'.

Morphological Analysis is a purely mechanistic way of generating problems whose solution might lead to advances in a given area of technology or product design. Once again the development problem is first thoroughly described – this time by identifying all the parameters (we might call them independent variables) by which the problem is described. The parameters for a paint container, for instance, would include size, shape, material and type of closure. Each of these parameters is then subdivided into every possible form: the parameter 'size' would include $\frac{1}{4}$ pint, $\frac{1}{2}$ pint, pint, quart, gallon, $\frac{1}{2}$ litre, litre, etc. A chart or matrix is constructed with each parameter shown as a different 'dimension'. A problem having two parameters can be shown as a square with the horizontal subdivided into the units of one parameter and the vertical subdivided into the units of the other. A problem with three parameters can use a three-dimensional matrix. Problems with more than three parameters – as most have – bring us back to a two-dimensional representation, with columns. All possible combinations of the subdivisions between parameters are then considered for development. If we take the simple example already mentioned, of developing a new type of paint container, we would get a layout like this:

Size	Shape	Material	Closure
¼ pint	cylindrical	tinplate	press-on lid
½ pint	rectangular	rigid plastic	snap-on lid
1 pint	spherical	flexible plastic	cork
1 quart	conical	paper	shutter
1 gallon	collapsible	glass	spring-loaded stopper
½ litre		aluminium	twist cap
1 litre			

Even with such a simply stated problem, we have $7 \times 5 \times 6 \times 6 = 1,260$ possible combinations available for consideration. Not all are practical (a one-gallon, conical, paper container with a twist cap), not all are new (a quart, tinplate, cylindrical container with a press-on lid), but some offer possibilities for development (a half-pint, flexible-plastic, collapsible bag with a spring-loaded stopper which dispenses a blob of paint when depressed by a paint brush). Thus, morphological analysis gives a multiple view of a problem and, being largely mechanistic, by-passes personal blind spots, habit and prejudice.

Examining a particular component, product or process in the ways described can uncover technically fertile areas for development. But our interest may be more in finding if there is a need for such development – will it be worthwhile in economic or social terms? To find out, we can use whatever knowledge we possess of past and present situations to estimate what future demands will be. We can ask our salesmen to estimate potential sales for an improved gadget or system, and they will provide an answer shaped by an accumulation of personal rules of thumb and hunches – not all of which will be reliable. Or we can assemble what data we have from the last few years and establish trends by simple extrapolation. Lastly, we can try to be more scientific (and complicated) by investing computer time and energy into techniques such as regression analysis, which takes into account all the factors which can affect a situation and the variations these factors can experience, and from them produces an estimate of the most probable outcome. The more sophisticated the technique, the more accurate it is, though only when history can be assumed to repeat itself. As Chambers, Mullick and Smith (1971) point out, the more radical the change contemplated, the less reliable any projection of the present into the future becomes.

Of the many forecasting techniques available, then, the ones which are of greatest help to the innovator, whose aim is to introduce just that change which will upset smooth projections, are those which are based more on intuition than on facts and figures. Chambers, Mullick and Smith list eighteen basic techniques and of these only three are assessed as having good accuracy for two years and upwards. These are the Delphi method, which we shall describe in some detail; market research, in which the objective is to read the signs provided by the market itself and from these to evolve and test hypotheses about future needs and possibilities; and the 'historical analogy' method, which requires a comparison with a previous product with similar characteristics from which a forecast can be made, assuming a repetition of the pattern. For instance, the Corning Glass Works in the United States used the historical pattern of the market growth for black and white TV to predict the likelihood of success and sales potential of colour TV.

A fourth method, developed by Bouladon (1967), involves a systematic search throughout the whole area of a given technology (human transport in this case) for 'gaps', that is, points where existing means of transport are inadequate and opportunities are open for speculation and innovation. Using the factors of speed, maximum range and demand, Bouladon divides the whole range of transport into six areas: three, namely pedestrian, motor car and aircraft, catering respectively for distances of up to a few hundred yards, 100 miles or so, and 700 miles; and three, between pedestrian and car, car and aircraft, and beyond the aircraft range, representing areas in which existing means of transport are considered less satisfactory by users. Between walking and car travel, for instance, there are many forms of transport available: bus, motor scooter, bicycle and underground train. But none fulfil the need perceived by town planners for a mass transport system, possibly continuous, operating at a speed of about five times the walking rate, for distances of between half a mile and three miles. Again between motor transport and conventional aircraft, there are helicopters, short-take-off aircraft and hovertrains, but all need development. Lastly, supersonic aircraft for distances greater than 700 miles are still not generally available.

These gaps represent promising areas for creative input in a descending order of demand (the need for a mass transport system travelling at twenty miles per hour is vastly greater than any need for supersonic transport in terms of the numbers who wish to travel at these speeds).

The Problem as a Speculation

Now we must consider problems which lie well outside our present level of knowledge and achievement, problems which we might be able to describe in terms of a desired end point but which require steps to reach it that cannot be predicted fully from our present position. James R. Bright (1970), writing in the *Harvard Business Review*, suggests that technological change can be anticipated by observing the signs that precede the change, often by several years. He suggests that a technological advance is heralded by accounts in the press long before its use is widespread; its possible effect is evident from its appearance on a limited scale; its progress can be altered significantly by changes in social, political and ecological values, and the activities of key individuals who control the resources needed for the innovation; and development will increase exponentially over time once bottlenecks are removed, provided further barriers are not encountered in scientific, economic or social fields.

Many engineering innovations are based on the exploitation of some natural phenomenon which scientists discovered years before, but for which no immediate use was apparent or no supporting technology was available. The properties of semi-conductors such as copper oxide and germanium were known by 1900, but it was not until the 1930s that the needs of high-frequency electronics made them a more efficient alternative to vacuum-tube rectifiers. The principle of jet propulsion has been known for 2,000 years at least. Hero of Alexandria described a steam-driven machine which operated on the jet principle we use today for rotating garden sprinklers. But it was not until the 1930s that

Whittle succeeded in developing the jet engine, because it needed materials previously not available to withstand the combination of stress and temperature experienced in its operation.

Things have however speeded up considerably now – as North and Pyke (1969) say, it is expected that '80 per cent of all the major scientific discoveries and inventions that will be well-known forty-five years from now will have occurred during the professional career of this year's college graduate'. A dip into some of the forward looking journals might give us clues as to the likely runners in tomorrow's technology:

High-temperature plastics

... Plastics have been developed that resist temperatures as high as 900°C.

N. W. Ashcroft in *Scientific American*, July 1969, p. 96

Acoustical holography

... By 'illuminating' an object with pure tones of sound instead of with a beam of coherent light one can create acoustical holograms that become three-dimensional pictures when viewed by laser light.

Alexander F. Metherell in *Scientific American*, October 1969, p. 36

Superconducting machines

... Their attractive performance and economics promise to revolutionize the whole field of large and powerful direct current electric motors and generators by 1975.

A. D. Appleton in *Science Journal*, April 1969, p. 41

Amorphous semiconductor switching

... Solid-state devices that are glassy rather than crystalline can be employed to control the flow of electric current.

H. K. Henisch in *Scientific American*, November 1969, p. 30

Photon echoes

... Experiments in which two light pulses are aimed at one end of a ruby crystal and three light pulses are detected emerging from the other end are explained in terms of the crystal's inherent 'phase memory'.

Sven R. Hartmann in *Scientific American*, April 1968, p. 32

Reverse osmosis: cheaper food, purer water

... Developed originally as a method of removing salt from
sea-water, reverse osmosis is finding other uses – from concentration of foodstuffs to purification of effluent.

Olga Illner-Paine in *Science Journal*, December 1970, p. 53

Superplasticity

... For thirty-five years scientists have experimented with alloys
that can be stretched up to 2,000 per cent without breaking.
Today such materials are about to be used.

Oleg D. Sherby in *Science Journal*, June 1969, p. 75

The heat pipe

... A pipe containing a wick transfers heat better than the best
metal conductor.

G. Yale Eastman in *Scientific American*, May 1968, p. 38

Salt-water agriculture

... Experiments in Israel indicate that many plants can be
irrigated with salty water, even at oceanic strength, if they are
in sandy soil. The technique might open much barren land to
agriculture.

Hugh Boyko in *Scientific American*, March 1967, p. 89

A solid-state source of microwaves

... A tiny crystal of gallium arsenide can be made to emit
microwaves simply by applying a steady voltage across it. This
phenomenon, known as the Gunn effect, may revolutionize
microwave technology.

Raymond Bowyers in *Scientific American*, August 1966, p. 22

Which of these will lead to significant practical developments
in the future, and which will remain scientific curiosities? And
how can we distinguish one from the other, the true signals from
the background noise? There is no certain and satisfactory answer
to either question, but the odds can be shortened by increasing
sensitivity to signs throughout the total environment in which
each phenomenon exists. Bright suggests several relevant areas:

The technological – trends in costs, size, reliability and availability of components likely to be associated with any development of the phenomenon; bursts of interest in specific topics within industry and professional institutions; new patents, learned papers and advertising literature.

The economic – industrial investments and government support for research and development programmes.

The social – population trends as indicators of needs, studies of leisure activities, education, disease, crime, poverty and pollution; measures of public opinion.

The political – government debates, committees and recommendations; changes in the law; the appointment of certain individuals to influential posts.

Bright coins the phrase 'monitoring the environment' to include much more than just sifting through the scientific journals. Any signal of change should be examined for possible consequences, the dimensions of the examination being carefully chosen and the information gathered in such a way as to be of greatest use for management decisions. He notes the tendency for investigations to concentrate solely on economic and technical factors even when it is the social or political areas which will determine the fate of a particular innovation. He stresses the need for an approach in which the widest possible view of the whole situation is taken. This approach should pick up both isolated bits of scientific discovery and exploitable knowledge from the developing areas of established technology.

Timeliness is an important ingredient in finding and tackling a problem, as we have observed. But how can we predict when a problem is likely to be ripe for solution in the years still to come? Bright does not offer much assistance: indeed there is little more than inspired guesswork to help us as we peer into the future. Your guess may not be quite as good as mine, however, if I am an expert in the area of study and you are not. This is the principle underlying the Delphi method of prediction. An excellent account of this method is given by North and Pyke (1969). In a study they did for T.R.W. Inc., a large American company engaged on advanced work in aerospace, electronics, instrumentation, etc., in which rapid developments are expected, North and Pyke looked at developments in technology over the next twenty years which might have a significant impact on the company's products, services and processes. A panel of experts specializing in different parts of the company's business identified over 400 developments. These were categorized and refined and then introduced to panels of experts in the various technical categories. Each member of a panel was asked to write down a list of significant future developments in his category, adding his opinion on each of:

(a) Its desirability from a customer's point of view.
(b) Its feasibility from the point of view of the manufacturer.
(c) Its time of occurrence, expressed as the year when it had a 50/50 chance of becoming reality.
(d) An estimate of the uncertainty which the panelist felt about this prediction.

All responses were made in confidence to avoid people influencing each other.

After further editing and clarification these developments were put into a new list and, together with predictions made by other panels, were given to the same people again to estimate the desirability, feasibility and time for each event. There was an added requirement that there should be consistency in the order of occurrence of developments, that is, events related or mutually dependent in some way should follow each other in logical order. A third round involving the same people was intended to resolve wide differences of opinion in timing by individual discussion with panelists, giving a final consensus on each development.

Having identified some interesting future developments and decided when they were most likely to occur, it remained to work out the technical steps that would be needed to achieve them, starting from the present state of knowledge. An estimate of the time needed to make each of these intermediate steps gave a check on the possibility of the predicted developments occurring by the given date, and a description of the steps and the state of knowledge necessary for their achievement indicated the technology which would then be available for general use. 3D colour movies using holography were estimated to be feasible for 1972, for instance, with accompanying improvements in radar, telemetry, photography and communications.

North and Pyke observe that the Delphi approach avoids all group discussion, with its tendency to distort through individual seniority, pressure from those holding a majority opinion, influence of the expert and unwillingness to abandon publicly expressed opinions. The method has its limitations, of course. It deals not so much with predictions as with possibilities. It cannot take the unexpected into account. It is not neutral, for, once voiced, a possibility might be acted upon: it could become a self-fulfilling prophecy. Nevertheless, any well-reasoned prophecy is better than none, and thinking about the future may reduce its surprises and give us a better chance of preparing for it.

What has in fact been predicted by the Delphi method? Gordon and Helmer (1964) of the Rand Corporation in America used Delphi in a pioneer study covering the next fifty years and came up with some interesting forecasts. By the year stated there will be a 50/50 chance of the following being achieved:

1975 – Weather forecasting will be at last reliable.
1975 – Education will be approaching the status of a respectable leisure pastime.
1985 – Medical symptoms will be interpreted automatically.
1989 – Some primitive form of artificial life will be created.
1990 – Some limited weather control will be feasible.
1990 – Rocket propellants and other raw materials will be manufactured on the moon.
2007 – A biochemical means will be available to stimulate the growth of new organs and limbs.
2010 – Direct linkage between the human brain and a computer will be possible.
2023 – It will be possible to modify the earth's gravitational field.

It is the aim of the Delphi technique to describe possible, but by no means inevitable, futures: there may always be alternatives which can be described now, or will emerge later. The forces which will tend to make any one of these prophecies come true will be in proportion to its attractiveness at a given moment in time and inversely proportional to the counter-attractiveness of possible alternatives.

A useful approach to describing a possible route from what we know and have to what we imagine and want is described by Kahn and Wiener (1967). Their 'scenarios', used originally in studies of political and military problems, attempt to describe a 'hypothetical sequence of events that would lead plausibly to the situation envisaged'. They concentrate on reaching some end point by a step-by-step process, each step being a stable and credible situation in itself although the means of moving from one to the next is not yet known. By producing different routes from alternative scenarios it is possible to see situations that should be preferred or avoided, branch points and best or latest times for taking decisions.

What remains to be found after such speculations, as already mentioned, are the means by which successive steps are achieved. Here lies the need, and the opportunity, for creative thinking to provide a practical path between these hypothetical stepping stones consistent with all known constraints.

The Input–Output technique developed by the American General Electric Company can be helpful. Although it need not be, its use has been restricted mainly to technical problems in which the input is energy – light, heat, electricity, etc. – with a desired output in some way dependent upon it. Whiting (1958) gives, for example, the problem of devising a fire warning system. The input is fire and the required output a warning that fire is present, with a number of constraints in between: the warning must be foolproof and continuously available; it must be quick-acting to minimize damage; and it must be discernible at points remote from the fire. The problem may not be solved in one step. A warning system requires several intermediate steps, starting with the fire itself and ending with some physical warning system. Whiting warns against trying to short-circuit any intermediate point – this is more likely to lead to a stereotyped solution, since it fails to consider the opportunities for branching into the alternative paths offered by multiple outputs generated at some stages.

The Input–Output principle forms much of what might be

considered the heart of a 'Systems' approach. This removes the limitations of a problem defined in purely technical terms and extends the definition of input, output and constraints to include the whole situation – men, money, materials, machines and methods. It thereby provides an overall view and allows us to arrive at a more comprehensive, unified and long-lasting solution than any piecemeal approach can make possible.

Thus, in applying a Systems approach, say, to a problem involving the manufacture of a chemical, we would not be limited to the technicalities of the process, choice of materials of construction, design and performance of mechanical and electrical equipment and methods of measurement and control. We should, in addition, be involved with the problems of processing and handling raw materials, methods of transport, and use and disposal of finished products; with the recruitment, training and working conditions of the management and men needed to run the plant; with the effects of the product and its manufacture on the local environment – the noise, smell, smoke and general pollution produced; with the long-term effects of our presence as an employer and a source of opportunity. Even then the list is far from complete, but we are beginning to paint a fuller picture of the total situation and thereby identify more of the important variables having claim to consideration alongside those of technology.

Clearly, the more complex a problem and the greater its potential impact on people, the more appropriate a Systems approach becomes. But it would surely be wise to consider all but the most narrowly defined technical problem in a context which includes the human element, if we wish to avoid unpleasant reactions and resistance to our solutions when we create them.

Jenkins (1969) suggests that there are four main stages in the Systems approach: analysis, synthesis, implementation and operation.

1. *Analysis*

What is the problem and how should it be tackled?

What is the nature of the primary system in which the problem is embedded and the wider environment in which it, in turn, is contained?

What are the objectives of these respective levels in the systems hierarchy? Are they stated clearly and are they consistent with each other?

Has all relevant information been collected? Have all constraints been identified (and all false constraints eliminated)?

2. *Synthesis*

What are the expected changes in the systems under consideration?

How accurate are the forecasts likely to be?

What models can be built of part or the whole of the situation describing behaviour, processes, operating conditions, etc.? In what form should these models be – graphical, tabular or mathematical? Can the models be manipulated to simulate changes in the system?

What is the optimum for the whole system? What system is 'best', taking all aspects into consideration with a proper weighting for each? How reliable is this system and what uncertainties remain?

What can be done to ensure that the 'best' system is realized in practice?

3. *Implementation*

Is the final design fully understood, its implementation adequately planned and its integration into the wider system properly organized?

Have the design and plan of action been 'sold' to users or operators? Are all changes understood and accepted?

Is there an adequate commissioning plan and a scheme for evaluating performance?

4. *Operation*

Have operation and maintenance procedures been prepared and put into use?

Is there a continuing feedback of operating experience to designers and are worthwhile improvements introduced?

Is ultimate obsolescence and replacement catered for?

Techniques of use in such a comprehensive approach include just about every one in the management book. Moore (1966) lists over thirty, including Critical Examination to get the problem right, Critical Path Scheduling to plan and time the project, Management by Objectives to define the aims of the whole venture and to get people committed, and Modelling and Simulation, Risk Analysis, Reliability Studies and Control Systems to aid design.

A useful development of the Systems approach is given by Nadler (1967). He suggests that if we can disengage our thoughts from the present situation when defining a complex problem and think instead of an ideal solution, that is, one which is not restricted by money, method or resources, then by keeping this ideal solution in mind, we will come nearer to it in practice than by trying to inch forward with the present as our reference point. Nadler describes three stages in the achievement of a workable solution: the Ultimate Ideal System, the Technologically Workable Ideal System and the Technologically Workable Ideal System Target. An Ultimate Ideal System represents the best system likely to be achieved through the development of existing knowledge. But it is achievable, even though at a later date, and can be made a target for improvement in the future, giving a fixed aim point rather than a projection forward from the present situation. A Technologically Workable Ideal System is one based on technology which already exists, but which does not take into account real-life restrictions such as money, available skill, etc. By designing several systems to this criterion and selecting one, the Technologically Workable Ideal System Target, as a guide, a recommended system can finally be described which does take into account all real-life restrictions.

Nadler quotes several examples which show the advantages of using his technique. One concerned two groups of engineers studying a fifteen-man die-casting production line in order to find a cheaper system. One group used a conventional approach, the other used the Ideals method. The first group concluded that a system using six men could be used; the second group concluded that the whole production line could be automated and no men would be required. But having reached this conclusion they considered the fifteen men made redundant and recommended how they could be retrained or moved to new jobs. Both the technical and human studies were completed in less time than that taken by the first group. Nadler adds that the proposals by the second group were installed with immediate cost savings and long-term goodwill.

We began the chapter with our feet firmly on the ground, looking for real problems within arm's length, and have ended up groping into the future and looking at methods for conjuring up what might be. All this is quite proper. If we ignore the debate on the spontaneous generation of ideas, then before we can be creative we must have a problem to solve. And it behoves us to pinpoint the problem we ought to be solving before we try to do it. Whether we are looking for the odd unsolved problem residing within the general limits of our knowledge and achievement, reaching out from the edge, or gazing into the unknown, we still need to gather what information we can that seems appropriate, to put it into order and identify the difference between what we have got and what we want. This difference provides our real chance to be creative.

4 Structured Aids to Innovative Thinking

In Chapter One a model was developed to describe the innovation sequence in terms of an interaction between the individual and his environment. We get a more subtle view by showing the sequence as a wave-like progression from the perception of a vague problem to a formal plan for implementing the solution. Fig. 8 suggests a number of alternating convergent and divergent stages: the problem is first brought into focus, then examined against a wide background, brought in sharp again to see if there are satisfactory solutions immediately available or, failing that, taken further out in search of something new; and whatever is discovered is brought in for consideration as a solution for development and implementation.

Each of these phases requires a distinctive attitude of mind and the use of different skills. At the start of the sequence we need sensitivity and curiosity to perceive that there is a problem at all, then the ability to stand back and see the problem in its true shape, to analyse it and judge the best way of tackling it; self-confidence, flexibility and determination during the creative phase; and discipline to carry the solution to its end. Those characteristics are summarized in the figure.

In Chapter Two we discussed those parts of the personality which support creativity, and in Chapter Three the methods for helping problem indentification. These, too, are shown in Fig. 8. To complete the survey we shall now consider ways of helping people to build up the strengths of personality they already possess, and discuss some of the specific methods available for developing the mental skills essential for the proper use of the problem-identifying methods, which otherwise might easily dwindle into unimaginative rituals without insight into their purpose.

We showed in Fig. 4 (page 33) a set of imaginary personality 'vectors' acting within an individual to support or block his creativity. From this diagram it is reasonable to conclude that to increase a person's creativity we would have to increase his 'creativity resultant' by developing those aspects of his personality which contribute to it and reducing the negative characteristics which diminish it. An equally important point is that the attributes shown in the diagram are possessed in some measure by very many people whether highly creative or not. Clearly here is a fundamental fact: most people have a creative potential, which

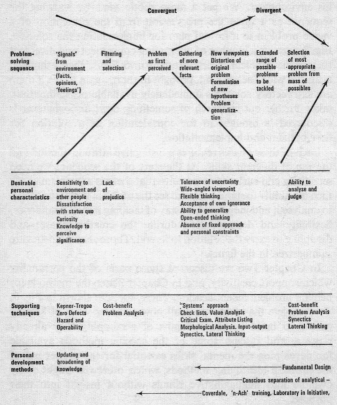

			Convergent			Divergent	
Problem-solving sequence	'Signals' from environment (facts, opinions, 'feelings')	Filtering and selection	Problem as first perceived	Gathering of more relevant facts	New viewpoints Distortion of original problem Formulation of new hypotheses Problem generalization	Extended range of possible problems to be tackled	Selection of most appropriate problem from mass of possibles
Desirable personal characteristics	Sensitivity to environment and other people Dissatisfaction with status quo Curiosity Knowledge to perceive significance	Lack of prejudice			Tolerance of uncertainty Wide-angled viewpoint Flexible thinking Acceptance of own ignorance Ability to generalize Open-ended thinking Absence of fixed approach and personal constraints		Ability to analyse and judge
Supporting techniques	Kepner-Tregoe Zero Defects Hazard and Operability	Cost-benefit Problem Analysis			"Systems" approach Check lists. Value Analysis Critical Exam. Attribute Listing Morphological Analysis. Input-output Synectics. Lateral Thinking		Cost-benefit Problem Analysis Synectics Lateral Thinking
Personal development methods	Updating and broadening of knowledge				←——————— Fundamental Design		
					————— Conscious separation of analytical –		
					——— Coverdale, 'n-Ach' training, Laboratory in Initiative,		

Fig. 8. Problem-solving sequences, helpful techniques and development

normally they may never develop, and in describing the personality of the creative person we are doing no more than identifying common human attributes which happen to be more highly developed in this person. Perhaps this simple approach does not fit the creative genius: there may be still something else as yet undisclosed. But the creative genius does not concern us here, except in the way we recognize and reward his special talents and his contributions to our technical and social evolution. As Stedman (1968) has observed, this rarity will invent under all

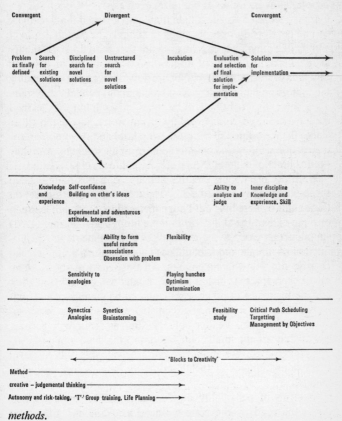

methods.

circumstances and conditions, and his determination, facility and singleness of purpose will carry him through and enable him to triumph over all obstacles. If they were all like this, Stedman says, we would have no worries. But they are not: 'Industries move forward as much by the efforts of not-so-great-inventors and through the creative contributions, large and small, of many earnest people whose cumulative work constantly brings us to new horizons.'

We are talking here, then, about normally gifted and intelligent people. How *do* we go about developing them?

First a word of warning. I am quite unconvinced that creativity can be developed in people along the lines of 'You too can have a body like mine'. There is no evidence that I can find of ordinary people becoming giants of invention because of this or that diet of words or mental exercise. Nor am I aware of any of our leading innovators crediting their success to some commercialized system. They were not taught how to be creative. No doubt they learned certain skills and rules to follow from others, just as an artist learns the techniques of his art at art school and the musician the theory of harmony and counterpoint from his teachers. And they needed practice to develop themselves. Guilford (1952) comments: 'Like most behaviour, creative activity probably represents to some extent many learned skills. There may be limitations set on these skills by heredity; but I am convinced that through learning one can extend the skills within these limitations.' Parnes (1963) supports this view, giving evidence of improvements in the production of unique and useful ideas by students attending special creative problem-solving courses. All this seems to show, as we might expect, is that just as people usually work well below their best performance in other areas, and can be stimulated to reach higher standards in the right circumstances, so they can be helped to use more of their creative potential. But, as Stedman notes how worthwhile are the small contributions of the many not-so-great-inventors, so also we should accept how valuable will be many small improvements in their capabilities, however modest each may be.

In terms of personality development, people can be helped along the road by the concepts developed amongst others by

Rogers (1961), Maslow (1954) and McGregor (1960). Rogers' theory of personality provides a framework for helping a person widen his perception of himself and so to know in which way he would wish to develop. Based on the belief that self-actualization is natural and everyone has some inherent capacity for development, the Rogers approach relies on providing a climate which will free the individual to become himself. It focuses on the person as he is and does not attempt to give him direction or advice. It accepts every person unconditionally as someone of value. The best source of information about a person lies within himself, and the idea is not to try to add to this information by providing new facts or frames of reference, nor to try to reduce anxiety and provide reassurance, but rather to offer non-evaluative understanding while the person clarifies his own feelings, increases his insight and develops in a direction set by himself. Rogers says, 'If I accept the other person as something fixed, already diagnosed and classified, already shaped by his past, then I am doing my part to confirm this limited hypothesis. If I accept him as a process of becoming, then I am doing what I can to confirm or make real his potentialities.'

To reinforce certain types of opinions or behaviour and not others is, to Rogers, to regard an individual as a basically mechanical, manipulative object, and he will act in ways which will confirm this attitude. Reinforce *all* that he is and can become, however, and the person will tend to act in ways which support this alternative approach. To illustrate Rogers' 'Client-Centred Therapy', take the case of an engineer who is successful, judged against the criteria of pay, status and the opinions of his colleagues, and who is sometimes sought after for his fresh approach to problems and his ideas for their solution. That is how other people see him. In spite of this, he describes himself as uncertain of his abilities and dissatisfied with his achievements, to the extent of avoiding situations in which his help might be requested. In discussion the Rogers approach would never contradict this man on his views or seek to reassure him by saying such things as, 'I can't understand how you can say such things about yourself. You seem to me to be one of the best engineers in the Department.' Instead, he would accept the self-deprecating remarks as being important feelings that the engineer had about himself and would seek only to show his understanding and to clarify the feelings that lay behind the words. In time the man might move from a concern about his failure to meet his highest self-imposed standards to the more important topic of his fear of taking risks. Meanwhile he may recognize his own resentment of criticism and his arrogance in forcing other people to ask for his help.

Rogers values man as a 'self-actualizing process of becoming' and minimizes the degree of influence imposed upon him by the method he uses. The same belief is shown by Herbert Shephard in his 'Life Planning' system, a version of which is described by Pfeiffer and Jones (1969). Shephard seeks to help a person to identify what he wants to become by first examining his life, his achievements and relationships to date; in short, to answer the question 'Who am I?' Then he is asked to answer the question 'Where do I want to be?' in terms of personal affiliations and fulfilment, to give priority values to these, and, for those judged most important, to decide policies which will satisfy the question 'How do I get to where I want to be?'

Life planning is not just concerned with personal growth, but with every aspect of a person's life, his family, friends, career, recreation and so on. In some ways it is much more superficial than the Rogers method, certainly more structured in directing attention to answering specific questions; but, by the breadth of its questioning, it is more comprehensive in looking at the background as well as the person. It provides only a skeleton design for development, but it goes beyond increasing self-awareness to the stage of deciding the ways and means of going about self-improvement, whether this be a change in priorities, a change in behaviour or a change in job. Like the Rogers method, however, it centres on the person and uses another person or people only to act as a mirror in which he can see himself. It requires a large degree of mutual trust between the people concerned to deal with personal disclosures from the individual discussing himself and questions and observations from the people filling the helping role. For this reason it will not work very well 'from cold'. At best it will widen the individual's perception of himself and help him to develop if he so wishes, and it will increase his companions' knowledge of him and expose more of him as a person and as a resource for any future mutual endeavour.

From the individual attention given in Rogers' method and Life Planning it is a relatively short step to the group approach employed in Sensitivity Training and the 'T' Group and experience-based learning courses, both structural and unstructured. 'T' Group training aims to give increased insight into individual and interpersonal behaviour in the context of a group. The group is brought together with no formal structure, leadership or agenda, and members are encouraged to express their emotions and examine their interpersonal behaviour as they deal with this disturbing and possibly hostile situation. By analysis of his own inner feelings and his reactions to the rest of the group over a period of time, the individual is able to increase his understanding of the internal and external forces acting upon him. His increased awareness enables him to take stock of his habitual pattern of behaviour and modify it, within limits, if he wishes.

Methods used to achieve this understanding include lectures and formal exercises, but primarily it is an unstructured situation in which the individual and the group can decide the direction they shall go and how much they will participate. There is no manipulation, no channelling of thought from outside the group and the depth of involvement is a matter for personal and group resolution. Benefits of such training include a greater awareness of himself and of other people, an increased tolerance of their point of view, greater openness to experience and a raising of personal skills in dealing with work and human problems.

'T' Group training has its origin in the United States and is not necessarily equally successful in a British setting. Roger Harrison, an American psychologist now living in London, with experience of 'T' Groups in America and Europe, including Britain, has observed (Harrison, 1973) that the European groups he has conducted 'seldom seemed to develop a great deal of depth or involvement on the part of the participants, and they seemed to require an inordinate amount of energy and skill on the part of the staff in order to make them go at all'. He concludes that possibly this had something to do with the different problems facing the European participants from those faced by their

American counterparts. Americans, he thinks, are 'rather more lonely and alienated, more disturbed in their family relationships, hungrier for a missing depth and intimacy in interpersonal relationships generally, and more willing to expose themselves and take personal risks to achieve rapid and satisfying connection with others'. Europeans on the other hand 'seemed less geographically and socially mobile than the Americans . . . frequently lived close to their own and their wives' parents, and they were much less often transferred between departments within their firms. They were thus securely embedded in a matrix of organizational, family and community relationships which appeared to meet their relationship needs much better than was true for most of the Americans. At the same time, the Europeans paid for their stability with a sense of immobilization, entrapment and a degree of importance within their organizations. They seemed more often dissatisfied with the amount of authority and responsibility they had, and they were more likely to express themselves in defeatist terms about the possibilities of initiating and carrying out change and innovation. To a person in such an existential situation, a group may be less a source of needed intimacy and acceptance and may rather have the function of encapsulating the individual and frustrating his individual growth and development. In my thinking about the problem I began to look for an experience-based educational method which would not require the building of a cohesive group for its success and which would focus instead upon the development of individual creativitity, initiative and action.'

His 'Laboratory in Initiative, Autonomy and Risk-Taking' was the result. The laboratory typically takes place in a hotel and lasts about a week. Participants, about twenty in number, are selected for their voluntary acceptance of a new form of learning and at the start are informed that the intention is to provide a learning experience which will be controlled by themselves. All that is provided is a wide variety of materials (books, articles, tapes, games, tests and exercises) which present a selection of areas for study, using many different approaches to learning. Members of the staff are available as resources on request and the only structure imposed is a daily meeting in which each participant must describe to the rest of the group what he has been doing. Some of the exercises can be done alone, some need two people and others a small group. It is the responsibility of participants themselves to recruit others needed for the group exercises. The prime aim of the laboratory is to give opportunities for each member of the group to pursue his own interests, each exercise successfully completed acting as an encouragement to undertake more demanding, risk-taking and rewarding action. This self-directed learning related to each participant's own difficulties, job responsibilities and opportunities, offers a powerful process for helping him to make better use of his own inner resources, and increase his ability to innovate, his flexibility and power of adaptability to the changes going on around him.

One of the sets of exercises provided in Harrison's Laboratory is called the 'Blocks to Creativity' and deserves special mention as a comprehensive method in its own right. Designed by three Americans, Sonia and Edwin Nevis and Elliott Danzig, of Danzig, Nevis International Inc., Cleveland, Ohio, it is intended to give an individual an insight into the ways he blocks himself from full use of his creative potential. It gives practice in removing these blocks and building more creative behaviour. The programme identifies fourteen blocks – 'Sensory Dullness', 'Fear of Failure', 'Reluctance to Play', 'Custom Bound', 'Fear of the Unknown', etc. – and provides a short essay describing each one. As with the Harrison method, each person is offered sets of learning exercises which he can use as and when he wishes: there is no set sequence and no timetable. To help him decide which exercises to tackle first he is given a personal inventory to complete. With this he can identify and rank the blocks to his own creativity. As with the Harrison system the sets of exercises use many different approaches and media and involve from one person to a small group of people.

Fear of failure, for instance, includes an exercise in which a person explores his level of risk-taking and his 'fear point' when carrying out a progressively more difficult task. He is given a pile of blocks and instructed to estimate how many he can pile one on top of another before the tower so formed will collapse. Then he is told to build the tower to test the accuracy of his estimate and to give him some idea of how cautious he is, that is, his level of risk-taking, which, if much too high or too low, can be important in normal work situations. Next he is told to build up the blocks again, this time paying attention to his thoughts and feelings as he does so, particularly when he first thinks his tower may collapse. He continues to build beyond this point until the tower does collapse, then repeats the process several times, paying attention to any change in his feelings as his experience increases.

An exercise dealing with the 'overcertainty block' explores what a person is sure he knows as well as what he thinks he does not know. He is told to imagine himself in a conversation with a wise old man who knows all there is to know about him personally. Playing both parts, the individual pushes the conversation into areas which probe his beliefs and knowledge by asking questions such as 'What don't I know about myself that I ought to know?' and 'What can't I do because I don't know how?' and the wise old man must give straight answers, which in turn demand further probing. After about a quarter of an hour's imaginary dialogue the main points are written down to help consolidate any new personal understanding.

No claim is made that the programme will make people more inherently creative; indeed the central philosophy maintains that 'the bridge to creative behaviour consists mainly in identifying and removing blocks to the utilization of potentials – capacities, knowledge, instinct, senses, etc., that already lie within the individual'.

More disciplined in its form is Coverdale training, organized by Training Partnerships, of London. Here the aim is to bring about changes in individual behaviour by a self-development programme which concentrates on recognizing and building on personal strengths and skills. It provides a series of practical tasks which are tackled as a group activity in a systematic way by identifying the objectives of the task, defining measures of success and encouraging co-operation and teamwork. Against such a background each member has continuing opportunities through discussion and feedback of results for examining his behaviour and bringing about any changes, as well as for developing his ability to work effectively with others. Usually residential and conducted away from the work-place, Coverdale training provides an informal and safe environment for participants to try out new ways of working and build up their skills in getting things done.

In discussing the personality of the entrepreneur in Chapter Two, we saw that one of his earliest motives is his urge to achieve. McClelland (1961, 1965) and his associates have studied this motive and its measurement, using the Thematic Apperception Test (Murray, 1943). In this a person is shown a picture whose content is ambiguous and open to several interpretations and is told to make up a story about it, including what has led up to it and the outcome. Such stories usually include much that is autobiographical, revealing the person's motivation, and his dominant needs for achievement, power or affiliation for example. When used for the study of the achievement need ('n-Ach') only, selected pictures are used and a special scoring system is used to enable a comparison to be made before and after training to increase this particular motive.

McClelland's method for developing 'n-Ach' includes coaching in how to think, talk and act like a person with a high need for achievement by making up stories which demonstrate the need, and setting rather difficult levels of success in self-challenging games such as throwing a ring over a peg. In such games any unusual personal behaviour such as a refusal to lower a wildly optimistic estimate of success is discussed to uncover the motive behind such behaviour – whether it is really to improve performance or to impress other people, for instance. All the time higher standards of achievement are encouraged in small, attainable steps and future goals planned to give a continuing improvement beyond the training course itself. The course is held away from the place of work and a spirit of support and optimism is fostered and stress placed on the common emotional experience the participants are going through. McClelland compares this spirit with the therapeutic atmosphere of such groups as Alcoholics Anonymous, where the group is sustained by 'saving' other alcoholics.

Having looked at a number of ways for developing those parts of the personality which support creativity (there are of course many others), let us now turn to methods which deal with the mental skills and discipline used in creative problem-solving. Four such methods will be discussed: Synectics, Fundamental Design Method, Lateral Thinking and Brainstorming.

Synectics, from a Greek word meaning the joining together of apparently unconnected elements, is one of the oldest systems for stimulating creative thought and has a growing following. It is a basically simple method, though it covers most of the problem-solving sequence, and combines many features of proven worth: a rigorous definition of the problem itself; separation of imaginative thinking from analytical and judgemental thinking; and group work. Its particular novelty is an enforced withdrawal from the problem and an exercise in free association which provides new ideas for solving the problem when attention is brought back to it. (Gordon (1961) discusses the method at length in *Synectics*. Other descriptions, by Prince (1968 and 1969) and Raudsepp (1961), for instance, differ in detail but not in essence.)

Synectics is a team approach. People are drawn from a wide cross-section of the organization in which the problem exists and selected for their interest and willingness to play a full part in the group. Five is an ideal number. A skilled leader steers the proceedings along the Synectics path. Success or failure depends largely upon him, so he needs to be a person of maturity, wide experience and optimism, well versed in the Synectics technique and able to maintain sufficient distance from the session to keep a balanced view, while remaining sensitive to each member as an individual. His task is to keep the team going along the Synectics lines but not to dominate. He may put forward his own ideas but must give precedence to those of the rest of the team.

An expert in the area relevant to the problem is very useful in order to explain it and evaluate any solutions generated against valid criteria. He need not take part in the session or abandon his specialist role unless he wishes. As an expert, he might be pretty rigid in his thinking. He has built up a framework of knowledge and insight by years of hard work and to admit that he is wrong or still has areas of ignorance might be too much to expect of him.

His likely reaction is to try to fit the problem to known facts and solutions. Nevertheless, Gordon says, the expert is the best person to judge novel solutions against a background of specialist knowledge.

The first step in the Synectics method is to agree on the problem. A group of people may see it in quite different ways. Their views can be brought out by inviting each member to describe how he understands the problem in his own words. This will not only give a greater insight into the problem but will also clear away some of the clogging effects of familiarity. This process of problem clarification and identification is likely to result in several possible solutions being thrown up immediately. This may indeed be the end of the exercise if something perfectly satisfactory is proposed. In any case, possible solutions must be dealt with at this stage, otherwise they may become blocks to further constructive thinking by participants clinging to their first ideas.

Assuming that the 'purge' of immediate solutions does not have this effect, the next step is to select one of the statements of the problem for further development. Here the novelty of Synectics shows itself. Instead of working on the problem, the leader diverts attention away from it by taking the group on a 'vacation' – a period of free discussion on a subject chosen by the leader in an area unconnected with the original subject. For instance, devising a new electric switch might be put out of mind temporarily by discussing physiology, the weather or marine biology. The area chosen for discussion is not random, however; part of the leader's skill lies in his ability to guide the group into an area which, though distant from the problem, can provide relevant analogies. Conceptual distance is important: areas that are too close, say mechanical engineering and civil engineering, will have too much overlapping convention and knowledge for a completely new viewpoint to be generated.

In *Synectics*, Gordon observes that biology is the richest source of analogous problems and solutions. Nature seems to have solved just about every problem we can think of, if only we know where to look and are able to translate the idea from one context to another. Evolution is a continuing, albeit random solution-generating process, those solutions which lead to successful adaptations to changes in the environment ensuring the continuing existence of a species. Search any area of nature and you will find working solutions to a multitude of problems – the homing abilities of the pigeon; the camouflaging abilities of the flounder and the chameleon; the firefly's ability to produce cold light; the near elimination of water's frictional drag by the construction of the porpoise's skin; a bird's ability to fly . . .

Another kind of analogy which the Synectics leader may stimulate during the vacation is 'personal' analogy. Starting with the statement of a mechanical problem the leader might ask members of the group to imagine themselves in the position of the mechanism: 'How would you feel if you were a motor-car tyre running over hot sand?' Such personal identification is useful for gaining more understanding of the problem and, by taking the individual 'inside' the problem, may suggest possible solutions as well.

A third, and in the opinion of Gordon, the hardest type of analogy to create is 'symbolic' analogy. The starting point is again the statement of the problem itself. This time, however, some essential part of it is compressed into a word or phrase – the idea being to summon up a word image which evokes the problem in a qualitative and generalized way. A problem, say, of improving communications in a large organization might be restated as the selective filtering of knowledge, to which the evocative phrase 'pass-words' could be applied. Speculating on this phrase during the 'vacation' may produce trains of thought which are seemingly irrelevant, but which when later forced into the context of the original problem perhaps provide a refocusing, from which a worthwhile solution will emerge.

Having put the real problem to one side during the vacation – which should last up to about fifteen minutes according to Prince – the leader brings attention back by asking the team to apply some of the ideas just discussed to the problem. Speculation is encouraged and suggestions for solutions explored. This is continued until inspiration runs dry or the discussion becomes repetitive. If the solutions generated are considered inadequate the steps in the sequence are repeated with another statement of the problem, other analogies in other areas and, perhaps, with another leader.

Prince is particularly firm in his insistence that all participants in a Synectics meeting should be supportive towards one another. He says, 'I also assert that the element which has done most to disrupt these meetings is the cycle of challenge, defence and counterchallenge that originates in the habit of negative reaction to a new idea.' It is very easy to adopt a critical attitude towards other people's ideas – in a perfectly gentlemanly way of course – and to receive the same treatment in return. We fall into this so often that sometimes we are not even aware that we are doing it. To combat such behaviour, Prince introduces a simple discipline. Before criticizing a colleague's idea, a member of the Synectics team must give at least three aspects of it which are good. The critic must review the idea favourably, thus opening his own eyes a little before attacking it. The fragile brainchild is given a short respite, maybe long enough for it to gain further support. And at the same time the member owning it is not so stung as to seek revenge or so put down as to withhold ideas in the future.

Synectics clearly offers a rich combination of disciplined problem clarification, 'method thinking', and support for individual risk-taking. As can be seen in Fig. 8, it spans the whole spectrum of development methods for creative problem-solving and, in addition, it provides a team-building process which creates an environment where creativity is the central and coveted attribute.

Housing the Synectics group has received careful attention. Not for it the plush trappings of the top management suite with the symbols of status all around. Simple, serviceable furniture in a plain comfortable room, a tape recorder (important for playback sessions for analysis of group working), sheets of paper on the wall for noting down ideas as they are drawn up; and all at some distance from the centres of power and conformity. This creates a somewhat non-conformist atmosphere, or rather a free one – free for the individual to experiment, to be wrong, to develop his ideas and himself. The headquarters of Synectics Inc. is in Cambridge, Massachusetts, and its atmosphere is in keeping with what the system preaches. The building still bears the marks of the stable that it once was. A spiral staircase leads from the ground floor to an upper room where Synectics teams meet to develop their skill. What furniture there is looks well used, and the whole feel of the place is more like a homely den than the headquarters of a high-powered teaching, consulting and practical inventing business that it has proved to be.

The Fundamental Design Method is defined by its creator as 'a highly disciplined form of thinking which a person acquires by a carefully organized and painstaking study of the controls which he already imposes on his own thought processes'. Edward Matchett, the British engineer who developed the method, describes the result as the achievement of mental activities of a higher order, higher 'not so much in the form of the logic employed, but in the quality, in the content and in the modes and depths of mental activity' (Matchett, 1968). We are all bound by the force of habit in our thinking, he argues, so that when we are stimulated by a problem which has something in it which we recognize from the past our response will be governed to a large extent by the mental approach we used at that time. We lose flexibility in our thinking processes and impose controls on them of which we are not normally aware and which can be quite inappropriate to the new situation. These controls will show themselves in our ideas, attitudes, values and visions as well as the way we typically tackle problems, and unless we can become aware of them by increased self-examination of our reactions, and do something positively to reduce or change them then they will continue to limit and bias our mental output.

To uncover these controls we need to create a model with which to describe our basic thinking process, a model which is absolutely personal and fully meaningful probably only to the individual creating it. It can be a diagram, chart, abstract painting, representation in 3D, poem or song. And even before this we have to ask ourselves what exactly is happening? This is essential but difficult for most of us because, Matchett observes, 'we do not, in our normal life, tend to separate the surface phenomena from their inner meaning. It is only by burrowing well below the surface, whilst at the same time monitoring continual mental contact with all the more obvious aspects, that the essence of the matter can be isolated.'

Some exercises are helpful in exploring our mental processes and Matchett offers several which can be used to stretch our approach to problems. These are best used and adapted according to the person, the situation and the specific problem. They are not to be used as a substitute for real thinking and insight. Jones (1970) summarizes five of these techniques as:

1. Thinking with outline strategies – sketching the broad picture before getting down to details; standing back to get a wide view.
2. Thinking in parallel planes – taking a detached view of the separate parts of a total situation – problem, people, methods, instructions, etc. – and at different levels of abstraction.
3. Thinking from several viewpoints – seeing a problem from different angles, opening it out by the use of checklists, diagrams, charts and matrices.
4. Thinking with concepts – representing in some symbolic way (such as described above for model-building) the problem, solution and interlinking thought processes.
5. Thinking with basic elements – analysing mental processes into identifiable elements (recognize need, imagine decisions, weigh and compare, predict, back check, scan, assess risk, remove obstacle, etc.).

With all this introspection and mental exercising Matchett aims to help a person to change the whole character of his thinking: 'It becomes much more penetrating and direct. It also becomes far more flexible and free from the conditioning of ingrained patterns of thought . . . Gradually one learns to become, as it were, an accurate and independent observer, and later controller of one's own thoughts.'

The method is not designed to provide a standard way of tackling problems and arriving at creative solutions. Nevertheless, the exercises and techniques used have been assembled by others into systematic approaches to problems. PABLA (Problem Analysis by Logical Approach System), developed by the United Kingdom Atomic Energy Authority, and MAUD (Methodical Analysis for Use in Design) and its complement PAM (Provide a Means Diagram), developed by the Fleet Work Study Team, are such systems. They assist a designer to approach a problem in a rigorous way, questioning each part in turn and displaying the logical progress of the design by charts and diagrams. But both emphasize the mental attitude needed to apply the system successfully: discipline, flexibility and awareness of the reasoning processes employed.

Matchett's Fundamental Design Method and its derivations have been accepted by many practising engineering designers in Britain and elsewhere, and real improvement in their work has been demonstrated. His concepts have been applied by people tackling non-technical problems such as communications and management. At least one major firm has involved its whole senior management team in Matchett training with the object of improving its general performance and ability to manage future innovations.

Some of the success of the training is undoubtedly due to the personality of Matchett himself and the enthusiasm he is able to inspire in many people by his presence. Others are equally irritated, even repelled by his methods. Like Marshall McCluhan, he creates a strong impression one way or another and like McCluhan he coins his own phrases to illustrate his philosophy. 'Man is poised on the brink of a massive move forward. He is just emerging from his acorn . . . at long last man has begun to take a hard look at himself and to face up to what he sees . . . the study of creative processes culminates in additional competence, and not merely in a changed method of approach . . . Ideally every decision that the designer takes would make the total creation (and not just his part of it) more meaningful. This may be beyond the power of man, but he can take huge steps in this direction where he is prepared to organize himself to do so. The machine or any other product of man's creative mind should be neither his master nor his servant. It should be a sensible and significant extension of his own being' (Matchett, 1971).

A simpler approach to creativity as a mental skill is provided by the third method: *Lateral Thinking*. There are two sorts of thinking, it assumes. One sort is most easily recognized when it leads to ideas that are obvious only after they have been thought of. This 'lateral thinking' is quite distinct from the second and more usual logical or 'vertical thinking' and is especially useful in generating new ideas.

Edward de Bono (1967, 1969, 1971), of Cambridge University, coined these phrases and illustrates the differences between them. In vertical thinking, progress is made by one logical step following another and at any point in the process there is a logical pathway back again. There is no element of surprise. Lateral thinking, in contrast, follows a path which is uncommon, not dictated by logic alone and which by its diversion from well-trodden ways may give surprising views of the problem and unexpectedly good solutions. De Bono compares vertical thinking with the flow of water along well-defined channels: the more it flows the more likely it is to continue to flow along these channels. Lateral thinking is analogous to damming up the old channels and cutting new ones to see where the water will go – maybe nowhere useful, maybe breaking out and altering the whole pattern into something suddenly simpler and more effective.

De Bono claims no magic for lateral thinking. Most of the time the problems of life are dealt with adequately by the actions we know: lateral thinking has no place here. But it is useful when there is no solution available, when present solutions are inadequate or when a new view of an old situation is needed. It is a mechanism for freeing the mind from habit and pre-conception and allowing an opportunity for wider, though disciplined exploration. Whereas in vertical thinking logic is in control of the mind, says de Bono, in lateral thinking the mind is in control of logic. It is skill acquired by practice, not a gift of revelation. 'Lateral thinking is for generating ideas. Logical thinking is for developing, selecting and using them.'

The techniques for developing lateral thinking include:

1. *The Intermediate Impossible*. To break the constraining effect of logic an 'intermediate impossible' is introduced to act as a stepping stone between the limits of knowledge surrounding the problem and the desired solution. Though untenable, the intermediate impossible must be related to the problem. Taking 'How can road transport be made more efficient?' as an example, the

intermediate impossible might be 'All road vehicles must remain stationary'. Ideas can be stimulated by this; such as having moving roadways on to which vehicles are driven and then carried along by the movement of the road itself, or having car transporters on railways (neither idea new, admittedly); or forbidding the use of cars at certain times of the day or week for different areas on a rota system; or providing means of personal communication as effective as face-to-face meeting so that travel for this purpose was unnecessary; and so on.

2. *Random Juxtaposition*. This is really another way of trying to find a stepping stone to a solution , but this time a random concept is introduced in the hope that some association will be sparked off between it, the problem and the solution (this is similar to the Synectics 'vacation' into an unrelated area of thought and the use of analogy).

If the problem is 'How to provide a cheap domestic central-heating system?' we might open the dictionary anywhere finding, say, the word 'nonsense'. Exploring the word evokes synonyms: absurd, meaningless, trash, rubbish, waste, etc. Rubbish? Could a burner be developed to burn household rubbish and thus raise heat? Waste? Could the decomposition of human excreta and other organic waste be controlled and the combustible gases evolved used as fuel? (Someone is already running his car on chicken manure by this means and sewer gas has been used for street lighting.)

3. *Searching for different ways of looking at things*. Closely analogous to Critical Examination and the use of a systematic approach to problem clarification is this method of de Bono's for gaining a new viewpoint of a problem. Stating it in terms of the purpose the solution is intended to fulfil, each part is challenged in turn.

'To provide a constant supply of fresh water on demand to domestic and industrial users' might be the purpose of a water supply authority. Challenging it systematically we could say: 'Provide' – why provide at all? why from the present source? 'Constant' – need it be constant? 'Fresh' – are our present standards too low, or too high? And so on. Rotating attention around the problem in this way gives a better appreciation of all its aspects and perhaps stimulates ideas for change. Challenging 'fresh' might lead to ideas about two levels of purity. Local water-treatment systems might be considered for purifying waste water up to some acceptable, though non-potable standard for recirculation to industrial users. Or a campaign might be considered for encouraging the collection of rain water for use in the garden.

Further thoughts by de Bono on the development of lateral thinking as a skill include the warning not to take the problem as given for granted; to clarify just what the essentials are, to find out which constraints are inescapable, to put the problem in its wider context, and not to be dominated by familiar and apparently successful ideas.

The fourth method for discussion is the oldest and simplest. As early as 1938, Alex Osborn was organizing groups of people to contribute ideas for solving a problem by insisting that they observed some simple rules which allowed spontaneous expression. From this experience came the technique now known as *Brainstorming*, which, when being practised, requires that:

1. No criticism of any idea should be allowed. Judgement must be withheld until later.
2. All ideas should be welcomed, however wild or frivolous.
3. The production of the greatest number of ideas should be urged.
4. Building on ideas to create a group chain reaction should be encouraged.

By insisting on these rules Osborn aims for a relaxed environment in which it is 'safe' for people to think freely and adventurously. Ideas cannot be destroyed since analysis and judgement are expressly forbidden, the more ideas that are generated the better – hence the greater the likelihood of a novel idea coming out – and it is possible to take other people's ideas and improve on them with full approval. A healthy rivalry in the production of ideas can develop, and since all ideas are 'right' in the context of the meeting there is immediate and continuing reinforcement to continuing their production.

Osborn (1953) gives further hints on the preparation for a brainstorming session. The problem to be tackled must be stated clearly and simply: multiple problems will lead to mind-wandering and failure to delve deeply into any one part. Advance notice of the problem will help people to tune in to it and to come primed with ideas. A balanced team should be formed, with a leader experienced in the technique and able to maintain the special discipline needed, a reporter whose task it is to record all ideas, and a few self-starters to get the session going. About a dozen people is suggested as the best number to form the team, with plenty of variety of background and some expertise in the subject among them. However, too wide a difference in status in the group may inhibit free expression.

The session itself should be kept informal but with the rules firmly applied. Clique formation must be avoided and a unified, collaborating group built up. Before attempting the main problem, a short practice session can be arranged, especially if a number of the participants are new to the techniques. A time limit of, say, half an hour should be placed on the session and used as a spur to achieve a certain number of ideas in that time. When people come ready with lists of ideas they should only be allowed to offer one at a time, so that the other participants can have the opportunity of building on each one separately.

Brainstorming is useful for generating a lot of ideas for later development into a solution. It has little to offer when the number of alternatives is restricted. And it is only a part of the whole problem-solving process. To provide a supportive climate for the expression of ideas, all analysis and judgement of their worth must be suppressed, but only for the duration of the session. Later, all these ideas must be subjected to hard analysis and the best-looking ones chosen for further development into possible solutions. But during the session the group must have the chance mentally to roam free, to look beyond obvious solutions and indulge in a bit of fantasy.

Running wild mentally in this way produces a fairly regular pattern. At first there is a flood of ideas, usually pretty obvious ones which come easily to the mind. Then the flood slows to a trickle, but with a change in quality. Increasingly novel ideas are expressed, as though the mind is wandering farther afield and searching in less familiar areas. Sometimes, but not often, a real pearl will emerge when the flow has all but dried up. Sometimes, too, a break at this point and a fresh start will result in another burst of ideas of high potential.

There is much in experimental psychology to support this last paragraph. Osgood (1953) suggests that there is a hierarchical structure of associations between words; one word given as a stimulus for free examination tapping a 'pool' of potential associates, the frequency of selection from this pool depending upon the comparative strength of past associations. For instance, asking people to name as many four-legged animals as possible will result in names like horse, cow, cat and dog being produced first, and words like gnu, platypus and mandrill coming much later, if at all. Common, strong associates occur more frequently and earlier in the sequence. Similarly, asking for the production of as many proper words as possible from a given selection of letters results in a lot of common words being given at a high rate at first with a slowing-down as time passes, but a proportionate increase in uncommon words.

Brainstorming is one of the most widely used techniques for generating ideas. It can be used for producing information, or a list of unknowns or questions to be asked. It requires very little training for its use, but experience in brainstorming sessions does give some learning in effective teamwork which can be developed in other situations.

Fig. 8 on page 74 analyses the innovative sequence into its component activities and summarizes the various aids which can help at one stage or another. From all of these, is there not some comprehensive approach, some 'package' which, if faithfully followed from start to finish, would guarantee a successful and publicly accepted solution to any worthwhile problem? Clearly the answer is no! The sequence in Fig. 8 shows a very complex series of activities, from identifying a vague problem to implementing a final, working solution. Only a part of the complexity of the situation lies in the problem and its solution. Much depends upon the people who tackle it, the environment they work in, the readiness of the outside world to accept their creation, and the availability of supporting technology, cash and time. And we are still only touching on the factors then, as studies such as Project SAPPHO at the University of Sussex demonstrate (see page 122).

Even if we try to restrict ourselves to the problem-solving aspects of the sequence there can be no standard approach, for there is no standard situation: other factors still intrude. Every problem that is embedded in some existing system (and that includes all but the most trivial, which can only be isolated because of their triviality) is special, in some way unique, requiring an element of tailoring in any approach to make it fit. And the more comprehensive we try to make the approach the more we have to make it flexible to allow for this tailoring.

All too often we witness short courses in this or that technique which give a passing knowledge of whatever is on offer. On following it up later we find no trace of it in action. It has been lost through an inadequacy of real skill in applying it – not to mention a natural tendency of the rest of the organization to reject any foreign importation. If techniques are to be successfully adopted therefore, certain rules must be observed.

1. The techniques must be offered in the knowledge and expectation that they will be modified to suit the situation.
2. Merely explaining them is not enough. We must be prepared to play a continuing part in developing the skill to use them. This implies becoming involved in practical problems, preferably at the place of work.
3. Knowledge and skill must be developed in sufficient people in the organization for it to have sufficient strength for survival.

A service offered by the Engineering Design Centre of Loughborough University of Technology is an interesting demonstration of these points. Full-time courses in design and aids to creative thought to groups of engineers from interested firms are given. Members of the staff then act as part-time consultants to the groups on their return to industry. In this way the techniques developed in the Design Centre are transferred back to a firm by a significant part of its staff, and continuing help and support is given by specialists as the new methods and attitudes become established.

5 Environment and Innovation

In this chapter we shall look at the environment in which the innovator develops his ideas: the reactions he receives from individuals close to him and the company as a whole, and the attitudes of the wider national community. Looking at this environment through his eyes, what are his demands?

'Give me a real opportunity to be innovative.'

'Put me among people who will challenge me intellectually but will also support me as a person.'

'Listen to my ideas, and support them if they sound good.'

'Do not try to mould me too much. Let me do things my way.'

'Give me help, time and space, and give me access to knowledge.'

'Link me into the system and make me a legitimate member of it.'

'Show understanding of my special role in the organization.'

'Give me a fair reward for my successes.'

'When I fail, give me credit for my efforts and appreciate the risk I take in trying to produce something new.'

'Give me guidance on wider issues and in areas outside my competence.'

'Put up with my peculiarities.'

'Look beyond the immediate disruption my work will bring and assess its long term effect.'

The reactions to these demands will depend on whether innovation is really needed and whether it is really wanted. Encouragement or discouragement is the main factor affecting the whole milieu in which the innovator works. It may draw out his best work at one extreme, and inhibit it at the other to an extent that, if innovation appears at all, it will be despite the general climate rather than because of it. The most significant element of this environment is the attitude of individuals – immediate colleagues and the boss – whose example, personal support and encouragement are crucial in the development of novel and useful ideas.

The innovator must have a job worth doing, one in which he can make full use of his talents and provide an important contribution. However, since opportunities for real innovation are few and far between and many other people may be involved in developing the creative idea into a finished product, the innovator may find there is little use for him and his ideas. What is the result of this? 'When he gets one of his potentially creative ideas, he feels he would be risking his job if he were to suggest it; or he does suggest it, but finds no one will listen. Our scientist can't "turn off" his flow of new ideas. What might be the result? He becomes disappointed and dejected. If he doesn't leave the job, he may slow down, feeling that his talents go unrecognized. Soon he is doing less well than his unfrustrated colleagues. In this sense his creative ability is hurting his performance' (Pelz and Andrews, 1966).

The importance of immediate colleagues, who provide both support and challenge, is discussed by Pelz (1967), who suggests that a stimulating tension is created between 'sources of stability or security on the one hand and sources of disruption or challenge on the other'. Conditions of security include the opportunity for self-reliance and for the pursuit of the innovator's own ideas. These are fostered by identifying him, by name, with a product, patent or paper; providing 'multiple channels for recognizing achievements'; making sure that he has 'a chance once or twice a year to explain his work to a colleague outside his group; and including him in review sessions with executives or clients with the opportunity to do some of the talking'. He must be given some say in his work assignments; opportunities, through face-to-face contact, to influence those who decide these assignments; time for consolidation in a job; and a team spirit provided by good leadership and competition with other groups.

Challenge is found in discussion and disagreement with colleagues, who may have different values and use different strategies; by periodically regrouping teams; and by involving a person in a diversity of jobs which require new skills. Older men's interest could be maintained, according to Pelz, by tempting them with problems at the limits of their specialities and by offering them opportunities for refresher courses and sabbatical exchanges with universities.

Support for Pelz is found in the observation of Mackworth (1965): 'In general, the social and intellectual environment is of much greater importance than physical surroundings'; and of Knapp (1963): 'Two factors showed significant linear correlations with output of scientists: the esprit de corps of the department, as manifest both in the warmth of human relations and contacts; and the severity of academic standards. One emerges with a picture of the successful department as being characterized by a warm but demanding intellectual environment. Material aspects of the department, including libraries, seem of much less importance and frequently showed a parabolic relation to productiveness.'

The importance of high-quality leadership is stressed by Pelz: performance is good, he says, when people have a sense of belonging to a group headed by a competent chief. Providing they have some freedom to make decisions, young scientists show rising performance with increasing intensity of interaction with their supervisors, although, Pelz adds, older scientists show no such relationship. Of importance, too, is what Lasswell (1959) calls a 'resonant relationship' between the innovator and a person of similar skill and enlightenment. McPherson (1965) develops the idea of a productive partnership between the 'ideator' who produces the ideas and a 'sifter' who picks out the best of them, gets them developed and protects the ideator from criticism. Such partnerships, McPherson says, are based on mutual respect and trust, the creative partner benefiting particularly from the stimulation provided by the other and the opportunity given him to discuss his ideas with someone, who, while understanding them, will not steal them.

While he profits from the opportunity to discuss his ideas, the innovator also needs the satisfaction of seeing them adopted, preferably immediately. But radically new ideas are more likely to meet with delay or downright opposition. Suggestion schemes in industry often fall down through the lack of enthusiasm shown

by supervisors to other people's ideas: there is a strong tendency
to put the suggestion aside for attention at some later time, or to
seek some flaw which would make it easy to reject. We have
developed many subtle ways of killing ideas. Who has not heard
(and used) the following phrases?

'We are not quite ready for that.'

'Has anyone else tried it?'

'Can you guarantee that it will work?'

'We tried something like that before and it didn't work.'

'It is a good idea, but . . .'

'We must form a committee to study that.'

'It's too expensive.'

'I didn't expect something like that from you!'

Or we just don't hear the idea at all, as it creeps out, faltering
and ill-formed – especially if it is voiced by a junior employee not
blessed with the respectability of appropriate background and
experience. The higher the status of the speaker the more we are
open to his suggestions. It is remarkable to see how a committee
will go off in full cry after some idea put forward by the chairman,
while a gem from the little man at the bottom of the table dis-
appears without a trace.

Most insidious of all, however, is the assumption that somebody else's idea can't be any good. I was invited to attend a
meeting by a group of engineers whose task was to find new uses
for a product. The leader was a man of proven ability and considerable inventive skill; so was each member of the team, which
met periodically to assess ideas generated and agree on those to be
developed. The meeting seemed to follow a set procedure, the
leader putting forward his ideas and everyone agreeing they were
good and should be developed. In turn everybody else put forward
their ideas, which the leader heard with courtesy and attention,
and then quietly and sorrowfully tore to pieces. Some of the people
had got the message better than the rest: they laid their offerings
on the altar and wielded the knife themselves. Afterwards the
leader was very sad. He had a fine bunch of people, he said, but
they just didn't come up with any worthwhile ideas!

Not many of us are heroes. We don't stand up very well to the
contempt and ridicule of our colleagues, and the chance of

bringing these down on us from on high is enough to keep our minds suitably disciplined and our mouths tightly shut. Once bitten, twice shy.

Should freedom be total? There is evidence that complete freedom is not conducive to high performance, except for the very few who achieve it by succeeding as the head of their own organization. (We shall describe some notable examples of this special breed in Chapter Seven, confining ourselves for the moment to the majority who have to work under conditions of greater restraints.) For the majority, what is the best level of freedom? Using the number of patents produced as a yardstick, Pelz and Andrews found that engineers in development-oriented laboratories performed well when they set their goals mainly by themselves or in conjunction with their supervisors. One firm gave a measure of responsibility to individuals by defining the general problem and leaving them to work out their own detailed procedures. Continuing interest was shown in their work in all cases, however, by periodic discussions with their chief and colleagues; such meetings providing opportunities for testing and sharpening ideas without the threat of veto. A general conclusion reached by Pelz and Andrews and worthy of note in support of the innovator's cry for some freedom, limited though it may be, was that performance was poor when the supervisor gave sole and continued direction to his subordinates.

Passive acceptance of too much control is not the hallmark of the true innovator anyway. Externally imposed structure and pressure certainly does inhibit some people (Maddi, 1965) – children and adolescents whose personalities and experience are not sufficiently developed to allow them much independence of people and events around them. But adults who need a wholly benign environment will be too vulnerable to be creative, regardless of their innate ability.

The level of control and interaction with colleagues, then, is important up to a point, and in general the effect of the social and intellectual environment is greater than that of the physical surroundings in which the innovator works. He still needs practical help, however, to keep him free from distraction and allow him to apply himself wholly to the job in hand, to provide opportunities for trying out his ideas (a workshop, materials, skilled help, etc.), reasonably comfortable surroundings (he may be almost oblivious to them, but even he will lose his concentration if conditions are too bad) and access to information and opportunities for speedy learning whenever he needs them. A place that can be used habitually for thinking and developing ideas, somewhere that will become steeped in memories of past problem-solving activities and is well stocked with books, articles and other relevant material is what he needs. Such a place offers a background which the innovator can drop into to achieve a continuity and style of thinking important to his work.

Acceptance of innovation as a legitimate activity – providing that indeed it is – and of the innovator as a useful though special person among his colleagues are reasonable demands from his point of view. They are not so easily satisfied, for in every innovation there is a hint of threat. Every new idea displaces something, somehow, from a position previously held. A new product challenges an old one, and maybe the jobs going with it. A new method requires new skills – skills we may not possess and which we may be incapable of learning. It may alter our status among colleagues. It may endanger our way of life. The further any new concept is from our present limit of knowledge and experience the greater the effort we have to expend in adjusting to it; reshaping our boundaries, struggling with incompatibilities between the old and new, discarding the familiar in favour of the unfamiliar, and so on. It is no wonder that the more novel the idea, the more we tend to reject it.

A celebrated example of people's opposition to innovations that are too foreign to existing experience is given by the fate of the warship *Wampanoag*, described by Morrison (1966). This craft was introduced into the U.S. Navy a hundred years ago with a steam engine as its main source of power. It behaved perfectly for a year, but was roundly condemned by a naval board called upon to assess its worth, for no better reason than it was too different from the conventional craft of the day.

Hence, ready acceptance of the innovator among people whose immediate interest is stability cannot be taken for granted. Visible support and protection for him from someone in authority, preferably his immediate superior, will be his best hope. An example set by such an influential figure will encourage him and be seen by the rest of his colleagues as a challenge to their own attitudes and behaviour. In time he may find a more general ownership of his aims and the attendant risk, and be able to develop easier personal relationships as he works to achieve them.

Part of the general attitude he desires is a willingness on his colleagues' part to give him his just due for his contribution to the overall success of the organization. Financial reward of course should be given. But the innovator does not live by bread alone: as Pelz and Andrews have said, he gets satisfaction out of talking about his work to others who can appreciate it, writing papers explaining it for the journals of learned societies and seeing his name on patent specifications. Enthusiasm for his work and acclaim for him as a person are true rewards if genuinely given.

This will be particularly true when something goes wrong and it is 'back to the drawing board' again. Then is the time to give credit for all that has been achieved, for despite the setback advances will have been made, and the innovator will appreciate a little comfort as he picks himself up to renew the struggle. Failure, if properly analysed, may become the stepping-off point for later success, and the quicker the recovery the sooner things can be moving forward again.

By his nature the innovator is concerned with the overall success of his work and not just one particular phase. He needs knowledge and skills outside his present range, and linkages with the rest of the organization which can further his aims. He will thus benefit from teach-ins and seminars with people outside his immediate circle if this helps smooth the path of his innovation. He will see the value of a short stay in the accounts department to give him an appreciation of how money affects his work: an introduction to discounted cash flow will both caution him on the cash value of time and make him better prepared for arguing his case. A visit to a production works will remind him of the practical difficulties of manufacturing. A tour of a municipal rubbish dump may give him sober but productive thoughts about the ultimate disposal of his work.

We have dwelt on acceptance of the innovator for the work he does. Just as important is acceptance of him as a person, for being the odd man out is not a comfortable feeling. Most of us avoid challenging the *status quo*, as in some form the innovator must. We find it very difficult to overcome the values and habits that have been implanted in us from childhood: that it is good to stick to the rules, that what was right for our elders is right for us, and that to question these things is both ill-mannered and dangerous. Unable to break out ourselves, we seek to pull others into captivity with us. The odd-ball somehow must be brought in line. His non-conformity in habits or attitudes can blind us to the possession of his unique personal resources, and if he is odd in his dress, forgetful of time and given to peculiar idiosyncrasies he is not likely to be welcome in the normal industrial organization. To see a man doing nothing, or to find his desk empty when we think he should be at it, is disturbing. The reaction may be to fire him or, short of that, tuck him out of the way; perhaps even promote him to another department, or give him a job of such a routine and repetitive nature that he will just have to toe the line to get through his work.

On rare occasions, though, the right thing is done: he is given his freedom and the system is adjusted to allow him the space he needs to be himself. It may be necessary to give him a special title to show that he is outside the hierarchical structure and that the special conditions allowed him are not a precedent with which to threaten its stability. But he will have the satisfaction of being accepted for what he is, just as he is.

Asking for his work to be assessed against its long-term possibilities instead of its short-term disruptive effects is reasonable from the innovator's point of view, but is a wish which needs a wider involvement of people than his immediate colleagues for its satisfaction. The general policy of the firm, its long-term development aims and need to achieve a breakthrough will flavour the general attitude towards innovation, and the views of the people remote from the innovator will affect and modify the feelings of those close at hand.

Several other factors outside the circle of close colleagues make their effect in this way. We can represent the immediate and more general forces as vectors, as in Fig. 9, using the same conventions

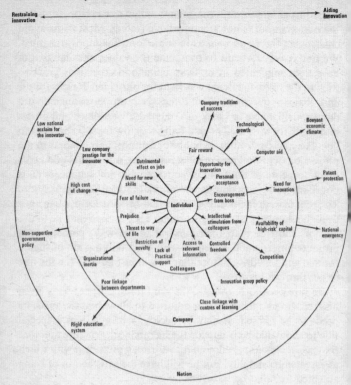

Fig. 9. Environmental pressures on the individual.

as those in Fig. 4 on page 33, vectors to the right represent features aiding innovation and those to the left represent features restraining it. Within the inner ring are vectors operating on the individual from his colleagues, in the next ring are those representing company values and conditions, and in the outer ring are the national economic and social factors which have some bearing on innovation in general. Such factors exert their influence in a diffuse way, and the terms in which they are expressed change according to where they are viewed.

An example of how the perception of a factor changes according to the reference point is given by considering the features at each level which contribute to the answer to the innovator's plea to be given the chance to innovate. At his own level it is satisfied by the type of job he is given; within the company it will depend on the area of technology engaged in and the problems that have to be solved; at the national level it is affected by political, economic and social factors, including geographical location, national emergencies such as war, or sudden loss of important resources and raw materials. At the present time, the growing fears over oil supplies can well be imagined to be giving general encouragement to work on alternative fuels and means of using them. Another example is the commercial environment, which is all-pervasive, affecting every level through regional development grants, the timing of public procurement, changes in hire-purchase regulations, etc.

A strong though hard-won strength whose effects can spread throughout a firm is a tradition of success. Recognized for its influence on men in the fighting forces and manifested by their behaviour in times of stress, it is no less powerful in industry for its effect on performance. The prestige and pride that is felt in belonging to a successful team can draw the best out of people. They approach difficult jobs with a confidence that they can achieve them, setting high standards for themselves and expecting the same from others. Success breeds success: the outside world recognizes special achievements, stimulating people to maintain the record of excellence already built up.

Competition also provides a spur to innovation, particularly in areas of rapid technological growth. Most of the basic scientific knowledge needed in these areas is already known, argues Burnet (1971), and is there ready for development. To this Sir Alec Cairncross in his Presidential Address to the Swansea Meeting of the British Association in 1971 adds that growth will depend upon market demand, the need to keep up with competitors, and the money and innovative skill made available – 'skill born of experience, of insight and perseverance in grappling with the unforeseen, of inventiveness and imagination in design'. Whichever way we look at it, the interval between demand and supply, or between awareness of the potential of a fundamental scientific phenomenon and its commercial exploitation, is much shorter today than it was just a few years ago. In Chapter Three we mentioned the long time lag between the discovery of the rectifying properties of copper oxide and germanium and their commercial exploitation. The ideas behind Babbage's computing machine had to wait much longer before they were needed by industry and means were found for developing them. Intervals such as these are now shortened to as little as ten years or less. Low (1968) estimates that the 'lead' time that a company can gain over competitors by intensive development effort can be as short as three years for small electronics products, four or five years for computers and communication satellites and perhaps seven years for the development of a big aircraft. Development costs are such that a firm must either decide to make a big effort to dominate the market or leave it to others to make the running, and be content with being a follower. A moderate effort will only lead to waste of money.

Technology is never in a state of equilibrium. The present position is always a potential stepping-off point for further development, though the direction may not always be clear. Shortage of a particular commodity may lead to the development of an alternative (atomic energy in place of oil and coal, for instance), or development along one channel may require matching development in complementary fields (high-temperature materials required for the full exploitation of the jet engine). Industries engaged in electronics, computers, space travel and plastics have shown developments in many directions, some almost unpredictable before they happened.

While competition within conventional industrial boundaries is the main type encountered, competition from companies which do not fit into such groupings is increasing. In the United States, a report to the U.S. Department of Commerce in 1967 points out that competition to the cotton and wool trade has come from the chemical industry in the form of synthetic fibres; the aerospace and electrical manufacturing industries have encroached firmly into high-speed ground transportation; and the development of electrostatic copying has been carried out outside the office-equipment industry.

At the company level, encouragement for innovation is shown in the amount of cash provided for research and the procedure the innovator must go through to get it. There is a natural reluctance to back hairbrained ideas and it is prudent and reasonable to ask for a description of the idea, its practical use and potential market before putting money into it. But however much he may wish to comply, the innovator must always leave a gap in his account which can only be filled with faith. Figures can never be produced to prove success before the event, and there is always the risk of losing money or having to spend much more than was ever estimated to complete development and production. Concorde is a sobering example.

For more modest innovations, Katz (1967) has suggested a 'quick reaction fund' to be used for giving support to any spontaneous idea put forward, whether or not it is related to the company's products. He believes that virtually every engineering idea warrants initial support if the originator can convince his boss that it has merit and can gain his support for it, arguing that it is simpler in time and expense to do this than to subject each idea to a more rigorous screening. His experience has shown that with as little as $2,000 offered for development work on submission of a concise description of the proposed work and a time-table approved by a man's manager, less than 20 per cent of the people who use the system spend beyond $100. Most innovators find flaws in their suggestions or lose interest, he says, before that amount is spent. Nevertheless, they have had the chance to develop their own ideas and money has been made available while there was still enthusiasm. Good ideas are less likely to be lost by this quick support.

Where the company itself gets its money from to finance innovations is another problem. In particular, few small firms have the resources to finance themselves beyond the initial work-up stage, which may often cost between 5 and 10 per cent of the total cost of a successful innovation. In America such venture capital is relatively easy to find, depending to some extent on attitudes in different geographical locations, says the U.S. Department of Commerce report. The vast complex of innovative industry around Boston was probably fostered more by the encouraging attitude of the local bankers than by the actual amount of venture capital available, although small science-based firms met with a very good response from the banks. In contrast, bankers in the Philadelphia area were unreceptive, even though cash seemed to be available, and the number of technical enterprises in this area was small.

In Britain few sources of venture capital exist, and those which do are poorly advertised. The National Research and Development Council provides assistance for the development of major inventions coming primarily from nationally financed research, though it also helps in cases of private development where, without its support, the project might founder. Other organizations exist: the Finance Corporation for Industry, the Industrial and Commercial Finance Corporation, and Technical Development Capital. This latter firm has the specific purpose of providing finance for innovation; that is, for helping a sound idea to become a commercial success. It is interested in people who can conduct an innovative business rather than those whose claim for consideration is based on inventive skill alone. Investing at the rate of £1 million a year by the beginning of 1969, Technical Development Capital is the largest private source of capital for this type of development in Britain. At the London International Inventions and New Products Exhibition in 1969 about half of the exhibitors had been supported by this one company. The financial support available in this country specifically for the small man in a scientifically based innovative enterprise must be regarded as modest in the extreme.

Other resources besides cash are important in encouraging innovation within the company. One sort of practical help that can be offered is access to the growing number of electronic and mechanical aids now available, in particular computers, which remove the drudgery of repetitive tasks, and free time for reflecting on technical problems, for synthesizing and restructuring plans of action and for exercising judgement. They can also enable the innovator to 'converse' in a direct way on the incremental fragments of the problem as they unfold, giving immediate results and allowing a smoother train of thought than would hitherto have been possible. Ease of conversation is essential;

Mackworth (1965) observes: 'The great designers of the century will be those who produce computers that readily respond to man's changing thoughts. The automation of science will start when friendly thinking aids replace the present rather distant oracles.'

In large firms – ones with thousands of employees rather than tens or hundreds – specialization and compartmentalization are inevitable. Effective linkages between departments are essential to the development of an innovation – linkages for the easy flow of information, for the progression of work through departments from development to manufacture and marketing, and for bringing the right people into the picture at the right time. In the compartmentalized life of large firms, however, one department may often have a definite and jealously guarded boundary with another, and professions may complement but never overlap: a marine engineer is an expert in marine engineering but incapable of constructive thought in any other subject, a metallurgist can think of nothing but the properties of metals, a civil engineer works on footings and foundations, girders and structures, but never amongst the pumps and pipes he helps to support. Demarcation restricts the activities of many highly trained and capable people to the extent that they use only a fraction of their full bandwidth of talents and knowledge. They all know their place and the system expects them to keep it.

A large firm needs to expend a lot of energy in just maintaining its stability and adjusting to the disruptive forces within it, and it is small wonder that it becomes stiff and unwieldy in handling the sort of change that an innovation presents. The best working situation is one which is stimulating and helpful, yet not wholly comfortable. Instead, what is more often found is one or other of two extremes: either too much co-operation, support and conformity to the rule of not rocking the boat; or too much competition in the shape of jockeying for position and fighting for resources and jobs. Risk in either case is something to be avoided because of its added threat to stability and security.

The small, growing, technological enterprise on the other hand, creates a very different climate for itself. Its vulnerability is positively stimulating to fast action: survival may depend upon it. It is probably short of money, and of the many and varied management skills needed to handle the innovation which forms the core of the enterprise. What is not lacking is enthusiasm, commitment, flexibility and an acknowledged interdependence which, coupled with the risk the small company is facing, give it a thrust quite rare in the larger counterpart.

How to develop a small-firm atmosphere in a large organization is a recognized but only partially solved problem. So far as dealing effectively with technological innovation is concerned, the problem is frequently solved by the innovators branching out on their own and taking their ideas with them. This flow of talent and energy out of the company may result in its own impoverishment. To counter the drain, the company can provide its own avenues for the development of new ideas, by following Katz's advice (page 109) and giving modest support to the pursuit of technical interests, allowing individuals as much freedom as possible in selecting their areas of work from within the company's range, permitting some external part-time entrepreneurial activities or, if it is really concerned, setting up an autonomous innovation group with part of the stake in the venture held by the people in it. The stake can be variously in the form of shares, payment by results and directorships for the senior members of the group. Some five years ago, in the United States, 'New Venture Divisions' was set up by twenty-eight large firms to provide new opportunities and allow ideas to be examined and developed in a more supportive atmosphere (Mencher, 1969). And the 3Ms Company operated a product team approach in which a multi-disciplinary team was formed to work on an innovation in all its aspects and through all its phases from research to marketing.

An interesting and rather unusual example of an innovation group is found in one large company in this country. It is in fact a spin-off from the company which has never been fully re-absorbed and retains a high level of autonomy. Its success stems from its geographical location, miles away from its administrative headquarters in another part of the firm which, while acting as host, does not interfere with its working. Though the group serves basically the same customers, its objectives complement rather than duplicate the objectives of the parent department. Numbering only six in all, the group maintains an intimate contact with the customers, designs, develops and makes its own prototypes and hands over control only when mass production begins. It has freedom of action within an agreed budget and its members show a strong sense of personal responsibility for all it does.

Industrial concerns can also stimulate research in the universities to supplement or complement their own work. I.C.I. carries out most of its research and development within its manufacturing divisions but supplements these efforts in long-term polymer research with its central Corporate Laboratory. This in turn collaborates with Manchester University in financing, guiding and running a Joint Laboratory for Polymer Science at the University. Part of the staff is provided by the company; and the steering committee, which gives guidance on the industrial targets to be set, is chaired by an I.C.I. director.

Established firms, however, cannot hope to assimilate all the potential spin-off in areas of rapid technological growth, and they can recognize the fact by giving help and understanding to individuals who wish to set up on their own, particularly when the new venture will result in improved goods or equipment relevant to the source company's needs. If this is too much to ask, an alternative could be for local authorities or groups of industrialists to form 'centres of enterprise', as Coleman (1973) suggests, where a number of small businesses share common services such as typing, accounting and a canteen under the control of a full-time manager. Access is available to a board of experienced businessmen, a bank manager, accountant, lawyer and representative of the local technical college. Prospective businessmen have to satisfy the manager and the expert advisers as to their personal determination and the commercial prospects of their venture and, if accepted, are offered basic accommodation in the centre and some credit for rent and services. Advice is readily available and monthly reviews of sales, cash and prospects are held when further guidance is given. Coleman has put his ideas into practice with the formation of the Gresham Lion Group at Feltham, Middlesex; the products of the group include 'hi-fi', temperature control, motor-speed control and medical equipment, all apparently with healthy prospects.

Not all innovations originate in industry. A large percentage of the enterprises along Route 128 in Boston, as we mentioned in Chapter Two, owe their origin to the transfer of technology and key personnel from M.I.T. and other local research centres, stimulated by the encouragement given to academic staff to act as consultants and directors in industry. Spin-off occurred mainly from those laboratories working in areas such as computers, electronics, instrumentation and missiles – areas in which new discoveries are constantly being made with potential for commercial exploitation. Massive investment in the space research and defence programmes gave plenty of opportunities for starting business in these areas, with further help coming from a Federal policy of support for small firms by awarding contracts directly to them or by subcontracting from large companies.

In Britain we have no massive research programme in the space and defence areas, but, according to Ministry of Technology reports, we do have substantial investments in research into chemicals, scientific instruments, electronics, telecommunications, motor vehicles, aircraft, textiles and nuclear energy for civil use. Much of our best technical talent must be drawn into these areas, and, given the right opportunities and incentives, development could be accelerated by successful spin-off into entrepreneurial ventures along the lines of the Route 128 companies.

Close linkage with sources of new knowledge and development is an obvious factor in the success of the small technological firms in the Boston area, and also in other areas of the United States such as Houston, Texas, and Palo Alto in California. This factor seems to be confirmed by the Russians with the establishment of 'Academic City' near Novosibirsk, which consists of research institutes, a design bureau and an experimental factory (Amman, 1969). In this country Cambridge has its growing cluster of small technically advanced firms, and the area between Edinburgh and Glasgow, well served by five universities, the National Engineering Laboratory and the Institute of Advanced Machine Tool Design, has attracted offshoots from many science-based firms. The area between Reading, Newbury, Oxford and Swindon includes the universities of Oxford and Reading, Harwell Atomic Energy Research Establishment, the Science Research Council

Laboratories, the Atlas Computer Laboratory and the Rutherford High Energy Laboratory, and this could be a third technological growth region in this country (Whitfield, 1972).

Beyond the company environment, in the wider national climate, we meet more general factors which nevertheless mould the personal situation in which the innovator finds himself, not least by the life experience these factors have given him. Mention has already been made of the effect of a national emergency – war, or the sudden loss of a vital national resource such as oil – but this is specific and relatively short-lived, though dramatic while it lasts. Wartime emergency provides countless examples of accelerated technological developments in the ways of waging war and the means of dealing with its effects: the atomic bomb, the jet engine, radar, penicillin, to name only a few. In the United States and Russia the presence of competition in the space race has resulted in spectacular advances in the electronics, computer, power and control industries. With the removal of these powerful pressures, we may see a drop in support for the special drive for innovation that they promoted.

In less critical times the wider forces acting on whole sectors of industry to promote or stifle innovation are more diffuse. Greater or less importance given to industrial progress by government, through its manipulation of financial measures such as development area grants, investment grants, taxation and the support provided through government agencies, creates a climate which will influence companies and individuals in their choice of investment of time and money.

In the wider context, as well as at the local level, technological change and the disturbance it creates affects the public's attitude towards the innovator. It is only a matter of time before mechanization, automation and computerization take over the drudgery of most routine and repetitive parts of industry and alter the work structure and the pattern of society which accompanies it. Alternative sources of power or new, synthesized materials can play havoc with expectations for a continuing, familiar pattern of life for whole communities, as the coalminers and Lancashire cotton spinners are well aware. With all this in mind, apprehension about the future is natural and each technological step into it cannot but be viewed as a mixed blessing. Political measures which will determine the direction and pace of such developments by the control of money and resources can seldom be sensitive enough to avoid the human problems which arise from them.

Reactions to new and potentially disruptive ideas need not be uniformly hostile. Innovations in home building and town planning in this country, for instance, may be viewed with more favour than, say, innovations in the production of palatable protein foods from petroleum. Both may require comparable amounts of physical adjustment, but the mental and emotional adjustment required could be very different. Our culture, religious, social and scientific frameworks, and the different values they place upon aspects of life and behaviour, mould the way in which we experience the change which accompanies any innovation.

The social system also determines the prestige an innovator enjoys. A technological innovator in this country has to be exceptional to be awarded a knighthood for his services; Fellowship of the Royal Society is just as rare. A successful politician or businessman can expect a life peerage; a victorious general, even greater elevation. By maintaining a precedence in academic circles for the classicist over the scientist and for the 'pure' scientist over the 'applied', our universities perpetuate a social pecking order which offers greater respectability to the man who studies Ancient Greek than to the man who learns to design an artificial heart. They give Ph.D.s for the pursuit of knowledge, however irrelevant, but not for its application, however notable. We must assume, therefore, that in Britain innovation is not so highly prized as other achievements. We may need it, but we don't particularly want it.

Society, through patent protection, does give the inventor exclusive right to the financial rewards his creation can earn. For private inventors, who still account for 30 per cent of the total patent applications made in this country, the patent system is a boon, particularly when for the trifling sum of £1 they can buy protection for a year for their provisional specification before even having to file a complete specification for detailed examination by the Patent Office. In a way, however, the system acts against invention by discouraging work in the area covered by the patents. In another, it stimulates attempts to 'invent around' the original invention which, by the fact of its publication, discloses the invention and the basic facts of its novelty.

Reference has been made to the effects of our educational system on technological innovation. This is one area in which many important answers lie. Long-term interest in the education, training and employment of engineers would promote confidence in continuing government support. In Britain, where, as we have seen, the practical utilization of knowledge is still regarded as not quite respectable, such interest could help to put into true perspective the relative contributions of the pure and applied ends of the scientific spectrum to national wellbeing, and could affect the attitude of the non-technical population, particularly the young, towards engineering as a profession and creative engineering as a vocation.

University education in Britain was, until lately, for the social élite, and did not concern itself with the instruction and development of practical engineers at all. Whitfield (1972) contrasts this with the United States where, by a Congressional Act of 1862, Land Grant Colleges were established: 'the leading object shall be, without excluding other scientific and classical studies, and including military tactics, to teach such branches of learning as are related to agriculture and the mechanical arts, in such a measure as the legislature of the States may respectively prescribe, in order to promote the liberal and practical education of the industrial classes in the several pursuits and professions in life.' That country's higher education system has, therefore, been based on the need to produce men competent to deal with the practical problems accompanying its technological development as a nation, and public esteem has gone to those who put their knowledge to practical use.

There is a time lag of effect to be faced in Britain even when we change our system of values, however. Efforts to improve the creative abilities of engineering students, particularly those destined for development and design, cannot show much influence on achievement for a number of years: it takes time to change existing methods of training and pass students through new courses, and the influence that the newly graduated engineer wields is small for the first few years of his professional life. Nevertheless, it is in the schools and universities that students acquire their attitudes and expectations as well as their technical knowledge. Long before they move into the industrial environment they have been attracted or repelled by engineering as a profession by the picture painted of it by schoolteachers and lecturers, and by the methods used in introducing them to the concepts and techniques of the art. The constraints of convergent thinking and rigid analysis may have been imprinted and the childlike tendency to explore and experiment long since inhibited by the time the students of yesterday become the graduates of today.

Here again, a lead has been given by the United States, where, in 1965, a National Conference on Creative Engineering Education considered, amongst other things, the influence of the educational environment on creativity. It recommended (de Simone, 1968) a restatement of what engineering is all about, an encouragement to students to regard it as a 'noble mission', and a positive fostering of creative problem-solving in the engineering schools. To achieve this latter end, it suggested involvement in projects which brought students into touch with such areas of study as the formation of new technological enterprises, raising capital, selling ideas, market analysis, appraisal of inventions and opportunities for exploitation, management of innovation and the law and taxation as applied in this field. From this followed naturally the need for greater contact and working with other disciplines—law, business and social sciences—as well as with industry and government bodies.

Public acclaim was recognized as a factor for raising the status of the inventor, and the conference suggested that the principle should be used to double effect by offering outstanding teachers of invention 'travelling fellowships', thus rewarding them and enabling them to introduce their way of working to a much wider group of students. Teachers should be selected at least in part for their past engagement on engineering projects and inventive contributions, and their continuing performance should be judged on criteria which included ability in the teaching of creative engineering. Some of the country's outstanding inventors should be invited back to the universities to work as 'masters' with students on general projects. Reward and recognition should be given to students showing outstanding creativity and they should be stimulated by special courses and projects.

In the wider field, concern for the 'abundance of ignorance about the process of invention, innovation and entrepreneurship' in the Federal Government, industry, banks and universities led to a committee set up by the U.S. Secretary of Commerce in 1967 to recommend that a major effort should be made by holding a White House conference on technological innovation, followed by a nationwide programme for broadening recognition, understanding and appreciation of the problems and opportunities associated with technological change.'

Initiatives to encourage innovation in this country are less well publicized. The Ministry of Technology stimulates technological innovation by surveys of industry, diagnosis of needs for improvement and action to bring about the necessary changes, including financial support, help in export drives, forming joint projects to assist advanced production technologies and providing advisory services. Through its Design Council Awards and other publicity the Design Council seeks to encourage engineering design. The Council of Engineering Institutions Committee on Engineering Creativity works for a greater understanding of the subject and practical improvements within the engineering profession. A few universities study the subject seriously and carry out research, usually under the sponsorship of the Science Research Council.

For the future, the work of the Schools Council 'Project Technology' gives hope for a more enlightened and successful approach to the development of creativity at an early age. Harrison (1972) gives an encouraging report of the creative achievements of young children through developing their abilities to think of new ideas, to design and use knowledge in very different situations from where they acquired it. Children can learn the concepts of engineering, and apply them without treating them in detail, Harrison says, and their natural urge to create, change and control can be channelled into making things for the home (such as a means for opening garage doors), for the community (maps for blind people), and for their own interest (controls for a model railway). Such activities imply the possession of the necessary resources and skills: 'A child cannot create in clay if either there is no clay or he does not know how to manipulate it.' There is a progressive sequence of forms of creativity which should be identified and fostered, in the same way that we develop abilities in the literary or mathematical sense. A five-year-old will learn how to create slides in the sand of sufficient slope and firmness so that a ball will roll down them, but by the time he is at grammar school he will have progressed to building a tape-controlled milling machine for use in the school workshops.

In a way we have travelled full circle and are back to the individual innovator and his immediate environment, but this time we are referring to the innovator of the future. Leaving discussion at this point, we should acknowledge that it is a topic needing much more investigation and support, for it is in this area that the greatest long-term improvements will be made, not only for the stimulation of creative thinking but, as we shall see in Chapter Eight, for coping with the effects of this creative thinking.

n Chapter Five the forces, local and national, which affect the willingness and capacity to innovate were discussed. Let us now consider the group for whom innovation will be the main theme; its size, composition, working style, etc., and how it can be helped to achieve its purpose. First, what is an innovative group? Simply the group of people who contribute significantly and directly to an innovation sequence. It could be one man:

'About the year 1772, I began to endeavour to find out if possible a better method of making cotton yarn than was then in general use, being grieved at the bad yarn I had to weave. But, to be short, it took me six years, that is, till the year 1778, before I could make up my mind what plan to adopt that would be equal to the task I hoped it would perform. It took from 1778 to 1779 to finish it. From 1779 to the beginning of 1780 I spun upon it for my own use both warp and weft. In the beginning of the year 1780 I began to spin only, and left off weaving.'

So wrote Samuel Crompton of Bolton, Lancashire, about his spinning mule, a machine embodying features of Hargreave's spinning jenny and Arkwright's water frame. His machine established Bolton as the world's centre for fine spinning and marked a significant milestone in the Lancashire cotton trade. Working on his mother's farm by day, he designed and constructed his machine by night in the greatest secrecy in the attic of his home. He then operated his machine and sold the fine yarn it produced.

Crompton was a remarkable though personally unfortunate example of the solitary innovator, the man who creates, makes and sells his own handiwork. Even today a man can handle an innovation single handed from start to finish and make a success of it, though he will probably have to rely on the quality of his work and direct contact with the market rather than on mass production for wider distribution.

More usually, however, the innovation needs many more people to deal with it – ten, a hundred, a thousand perhaps (Whittle needed a team of 1,400 to develop and produce a few prototype jet engines). The group may have spun off from a large firm or academic centre, or have grown as a new venture within an established organization. It may have begun as a small number of enthusiasts trying to develop an idea in a small shed. Whatever its origin, the kitchen table, spin-off or a deliberate new venture, an innovation group must find the answers to many questions. Having a bright idea is only one step in the whole process of innovation. What problem will the idea solve? Does it have a practical and profitable outlet? Is it capable of economic manufacture? What skills are needed to make it and use it? How about competition? Answers to such questions, and dozens more, must be found and the right decisions made upon them if a new venture is to be successful. The talents, special knowledge and experience of more than one man will be needed to fulfil this requirement. Even when the innovation is no more than an increase in size or variation on an established theme it is probable that a whole team of specialists will have to be assembled to pool their resources and share in the project.

Forming an innovative group, choosing the people to give it life and character, developing it as a team, leading it and creating an environment in which to work all deserve close attention. Here the discussion will be directed towards the interactions of people in and around the group. It is possible to observe what goes on between people at this level and to influence it to some degree, particularly when there are some pointers which can be followed towards successful innovation. Understanding what the customer wants and paying close attention to marketing of the product, for instance, are more associated with success than failure, according to Freeman (1971 and 1972). Efficient development work, carried out 'in house' rather than by outsiders while making full use of external advice and technology, are also likely to go with success, as is giving responsibility and greater authority for the innovation to more senior people in the organization. Size of the group in itself does not explain success or failure, as Freeman says: 'Clearly there is no virtue in smallness for its own sake . .

the advantages which small size may give probably lie in internal communication, in specialization and in motivation.' It is to these latter factors, and others to do with the intimate working of a group, that we will devote the rest of this chapter.

If we consider any group as a repository of energy and talent, then our object is simply to identify and develop ways of conserving that energy for useful work and directing it through individual talents towards successful innovation. Let us begin by selecting a balanced group. All too often what we get is a collection of people thrown together for reasons of availability, job title or blind habit. Rarely is balance in human terms considered. Even more rarely is a group formed from people with a burning interest in solving its given problem, despite the evidence of the remarkable things that dedicated people inside and outside industry have sometimes achieved.

It is surely not enough just to satisfy the purely technical needs of the group by staffing it with people who have sufficient knowledge and skill between them to solve a particular problem. In order to form a truly multi-disciplinary team able to deal with wider aspects of the larger ventures we need environmental experts to consider the effects of the innovation on the surroundings, sociologists on the lives that will be changed, biologists on the effects on the balance of nature – not to mention economists, accountants, medical people and lawyers, whose voices may be raised sooner or later (and the louder the more novel the innovation). Furthermore, if only the sum of the technical competence in the group is considered then a number of personal factors of equal or greater importance will be neglected. Each person, with his inner beliefs and feelings and outward behaviour, interacts with the rest of the group. His 'life space' intrudes upon those of his colleagues through proximity and shared activities. The resulting jumble of overlaps of interests, attitudes, approaches and so on inevitably leads to modifications of individual behaviour when working in the group. In coming together to solve the problem the different members compete, co-operate, complement and in general aid or detract from each other's contribution. Having the right blend of personalities can make all the difference between chaos, stalemate and high achievement.

Some important differences between people working in innovative situations lie in the attitudes they have towards problems. There are wide variations in people's ability to recognize a problem, just as there are in their ability to solve it. Anticipating a problem, having a 'nose' for the significance of small signs, as we discussed in Chapter Two, has a similar spread, with most people at the low-performance end. Lloyd (1967) speaks of 'those rare ones – the anticipators of the world's problems ... How many people do you know who can – figuratively speaking – see around corners of time and event? Not many, I'll venture.'

Other differences with special relevance to creative work are the mental skills described by McPherson (1967) and others as creative thinking, analytical thinking and judicial thinking. All are necessary in the innovative sequence and should all be available in the group in sufficient strength at the right time. The innovative group must therefore be considered from the point of view of its intellectual composition as well as of its professional and personal makeup. Creative thinkers, analysers and those with a balancing judgement must be mixed in such proportions that the essential optimism, risk-taking and technical exploration of the creative component is countered by the risk-avoiding, backward-looking analytical component, and both are assessed and a realistic decision is taken by the judicial component, all in their proper time.

On top of all these complementary characteristics must be built a means of varying their domination in the group. There must be a time for unrestrained, wide, speculative thinking and a time for cold analysis. The group must be able to know when each style of thinking is appropriate and be sufficiently flexible to make the change.

In support of the preceding paragraphs, here are the comments of some of our most successful innovators. Alastair Pilkington has said: 'We take team building very seriously ... We choose the people for these teams in order to get the authority there; otherwise the thing can be undermined. You have got to provide the knowledge and the experience ... And we try to do another sort of analysis relating to the characteristics of the individuals, to make sure that they add up together. We analyse all the people and try to assess the total effect of the team. And we try to make them spend some time on analysis of themselves: Are we working together? Do we have the necessary expertise? Do we feel we are effective? Are we really persuading the people outside to take the necessary action? Are we getting results right through to the point of application, or are we finding that there are people outside who are blocking us?'

Alex Moulton, speaking in 1968 on 'Creativity in the Engineer' at the Institution of Mechanical Engineers, said: 'I maintain therefore that our present needs are best served by the establishment of creative teams of engineers. Of course, within this there must be one man at least to have the original imaginative concept; otherwise it will be useless in bringing forward innovation. And like any team it must of course have a leader constantly to reiterate the purpose and to hold the project on course and take the decisions day by day. But what in my opinion is more generally lacking and more needful of development is the team as a whole: the environment and organization thereof.'

And thirdly, Tim Eiloart, founder and one-time Chairman of Cambridge Consultants, said: 'If someone comes to us for employment, we test him very thoroughly. We have about nine points which we evaluate – creativity, mental ability, finishing power, company worker characteristic, and so on. We look for, say, four of those and if the group is a bit lacking in a couple then we would look for those two in him. We don't generally say this is a job requiring such and such a degree or things like that, because by and large no matter what the job is this month we might have to do something quite different next month. I wouldn't say applicants had to have degrees: we would look for high mental ability, which you can measure whether he has got a degree or not; that is his judgement, intelligence and critical thinking. We have had odd balls joining us who didn't get a degree; some successful and some not.

'What is important to us is a measure of a man's character as well as his mental ability. We don't expect him to measure up to any particular thing; we just say he must measure up well on a number of facts. And these must relate to the needs of the team. Our traditional way of recruitment might have been to take on creative people, who are generally not good company workers, and we would try now to introduce good finishers and good company workers.

'In a team there would probably be one highly creative individual, who would be balanced by the rest to give the necessary creative tension, but not an explosive tension.'

Having formed the group, we have now to develop it. Any innovative group, whatever its objective and area of activity, is going to live through change – of its own making to be sure, but no less disconcerting for that. Somehow it has got to keep its balance as it gropes forward, and not lose its sense of direction or momentum. It will need help under the four following headings:

1. Integrating the members of the group into a team.
2. Giving them a definite aim and means of monitoring progress towards their objective.
3. Developing an ability to adjust to change.
4. Building up a healthy relationship with the rest of the organization.

How can a group of very different people be built into a well-fitted, mutually supporting unit? If they are well acquainted and have worked with each other before they may need little more than a few hours together to renew old ties and rekindle the flame of co-operation. For all their past experience, however, we will be lucky if that is enough. At some period of time in the past they were in phase with one another, had pooled their resources and worked well together. But since then they have gone their separate ways, and have changed, subtly or grossly, in the meantime. James has followed up his interest in electronics and now knows more than Jack, who used to teach him on the side; Henry has married and is no longer prepared to put in late-night sessions; Bill is looking for promotion and would rather show his organizing ability than get down to the problem. And so on. If this is likely to be the case with the revival of a once competent group, it will certainly be so for a new group coming together without prior knowledge of each other as people or resources.

However, if we can discover how individual members view the situation and what fears and worries they have about it, we can do something to deal with them. This can be done quite simply, given a willingness to talk about personal apprehensions. Each member is interviewed privately, using some acceptable person as interviewer, the views expressed then being summarized in an impersonal way for group discussion later. Making the views non-attributable gives each person the opportunity to claim or disclaim any particular comment that he wishes, while giving the group the opportunity of facing it as an issue requiring some joint action. By this means, a direct personal problem such as, 'Nobody has said so outright, but I think I was in line for promotion in my present job, and I might have lost the chance by coming on this job' can be worded 'Will our promotion prospects in the company be safeguarded when we join this group?' Or the more personal 'I feel a bit of an outsider and doubt if the rest will accept me' can be put over as 'How can we make sure we make full use of everybody's experience and skills?' Really deep-seated problems and violent personal incompatibilities, however, should not occur if the job of selection has been done properly.

There is value in observing a group working on a problem, if it is followed by a helpful feedback of comments and honest appraisal by the group. Rather more confronting – sometimes to the point of shock – is a videotape played back for the group to analyse its own behaviour. A bit less extreme is a tape recording, with its capacity to reproduce the voice but not the equally revealing messages conveyed in non-verbal ways. The aim is to increase people's awareness of how they are behaving in the group, and the effect they are having on one another. This can also be achieved by direct but sensitive comment from an 'observer'. The person may be a trusted outsider, or a member of the group deputed to act as such; or members may take it in turns to do the job, to experience the situation from both angles. Whoever takes the role of observer must learn the rules for helpful feedback:

1. He must time his comments well, but the sooner after the event the better. His comments will be most helpful when the group is willing to listen; preferably when they ask for them.

2. He is not a judge. His job is to describe what he has seen, to mirror people's behaviour back to them without attacking them. This does not imply that he must be neutral. He has feelings and can help the group by describing the effect its behaviour has had on him. But this the members can accept or reject as they wish.

3. To be helpful his comments must be about behaviour over which people have some control. It is no good describing failures or shortcomings which they can do little about – they can't change their voices, their physique or basic manner – and comments on these can only cause distress or irritation.

4. His observations must be accurately and clearly stated. Inaccuracy will lead to challenge and counter-attack: bad presentation will fail to get the point home.

5. His observations must be specific. Telling the group that it missed several opportunities to develop ideas is not as helpful as saying 'When Harry suggested a helicopter instead of a crane Jim told him to grow up. Bill interrupted Ben three times when he was trying to describe his idea for a free-standing column, and he never did finish it,' etc.

The group should not, of course, spend too much time learning about itself and its individual members. Most of its energy will be directed towards the job in hand, and attempts to impose a regimen of continual observation and introspection will soon become very off-putting. Better to do this periodically, or to put aside time when the group can examine its behaviour in a non-routine context, perhaps when working on some very simple task. This is said despite some acid comments which have appeared in the popular press on executives and managers going away together for days to play games and build towers with Lego bricks. No wonder the country is going downhill, some say, when the brains of industry are reduced to playing like children instead of trying to solve the real problems of the day. Hard words. Yet it is only when the technical content of a task is reduced to a minimum that people's behaviour begins to stand out, especially to themselves. Giving a Noddy-type task to tackle diminishes the requirement for mental skill and knowledge to a minimum and places the accent on the personal behaviour of the people carrying it out. Undertaken seriously, the results can be salutary. This type of experience is appropriate to the group when it has achieved a certain maturity and is itself ready and willing to learn. Offering it prematurely can result in fierce opposition based on incomprehension.

Let us now look in some detail at two examples of group interaction. The first group, five engineering students, had been brought together by invitation after showing an interest in creative thinking. They had had no experience of working together as friends or project partners, although they were all in the same year of study. No time was allowed for them to shake down as a team and no suggestions were given on how they might work effectively together. After a short talk on creativity in engineering they were given the task of devising 'a means of walking on water'. No other instructions were given. After some mirth and references to miracles, the conversation went like this:

OBSERVATIONS

A Well, he said 'walking on water', so I suppose he was excluding simple floats strapped to your feet.

'A' imposes a needless constraint. 'Walking on water' was never defined, although different interpretations emerge . . .

B Yes, that would be too simple . . .

A In that case it's impossible. You can't walk on water on your two flat feet: you would just sink.

C I don't know, I saw a TV programme with someone walking inside a big plastic balloon on the water. They seemed to have some difficulty in keeping steady but they were able to . . .

. . . such as this, which seemed to hold some promise, especially since it was based on real evidence . . .

A The only way you could walk on water would be

. . . but A cuts in and the idea is not pursued. A is returning

OBSERVATIONS

using floats – like big skis, say.

D How big would they have to be to support your weight?

A And how would you walk forward? You would just skid on the same spot.

D Maybe you could put little hinged flaps underneath so that they 'feathered' when you moved the ski forward and stayed firm when you pushed the other one after it.

A How could you keep your balance? You can only keep upright on snow skis because the snow is firm enough to support you.

D If you kept your weight on both skis all the time you would be all right.

C Like surfing. Imagine the surf board cut in half length-ways – you've got your 'walking' skis then. If we knew how big a water ski had to be to take your weight, we would know where to start with D's idea.

A But a water ski hasn't got enough buoyancy to hold you up when it isn't moving. It is something to do with movement . . .

C I was on the beach some-where when I saw people

to the idea that he previously disallowed.

D is attempting to develop A's suggestion . . .

. . . but A is analysing it and seems to find little merit . . . although D persists.

A continues to analyse possible solutions before they are fully developed – but also provokes constructive thought in others.

C takes D's idea and builds on it.

A's analysis is again a mixed blessing: partly destructive and partly constructive . . .

. . . because C develops move-ment as a line of thought which with flat wooden discs about the size of dustbin lids. They skidded them on shallow pools of water and then jumped onto them. They seemed to go along quite well.

offers another channel of explanation: but it is not followed . . .

D Of course! That's how water skiers start off. They sink in the water until they are pulled forward at a certain speed, when they rise up and slide over the surface. How can we find out the minimum speed for this to happen?

. . . instead it stimulates D to follow the walking ski idea further.

A It must be faster than a walking pace, otherwise someone would have tried it already.

A uses a classic 'killer phrase' against the idea.

B Maybe they have. Who does water ski-ing? They could tell us.

C When they come ashore they seem to stop almost before they sink . . .

C contributes some very approximate but relevant information . . .

A Anyway the water would have to be perfectly smooth otherwise they would fall over.

while A adds a pessimistic note with an unsubstantiated opinion.

C If you could move forward by vertical movements of your legs, like riding a bike, instead of walking, it might be easier to keep your balance.

C counters with a direct analogy which is fact.

D What we need are little water pumps which squirt water backwards and push you forwards . . . Or if you could keep on falling forwards . . .

Starting with one idea, D seems to lose interest and passes to another idea which isn't finished.

OBSERVATIONS

C A porpoise moves by un-
dulating its body and tail.
Could we make a hinged ski
that somehow undulated with
a treadling effect of the feet?

C seems to be following his own
thought process with little
regard to the others.

A That's stupid! How could
you get going?

A continues to play his analyser
role

C These people you see scull-
ing boats along with one oar
at the back seem to manage
all right with a sort of figure-
of-eight action.

which C ignores as he follows
another line of thinking based
on analogy, but leaves it without further development.

A But how do you start when
you're flat on your back
with your flippers in a twist
and threatening to break
your ankles?

Nobody picks up the idea and
A comes in with another dis-
paraging remark . . .

C You could get started by
hanging on to a boat or
something. After all, water
skiers need a boat all the
time . . .

. . . which again stimulates C.

In the discussion, two students had dominated the rest; C with
his ideas and the other, A, with his attempts to destroy them. D's
contributions were positive, and though less than C's, helped
things along with his ideas for propelling the skis forward by
water jet propulsion and, alternatively, for increasing the 'grip'
of the skis when trying to move forward. B had little to say, and
E, the fifth member of the group, remained aloof and made no
contribution; nor did anyone appeal to him by word or gesture
for ideas or support.

A's analytical attitude was not wholly destructive, of course,
since his remarks seemed to provoke C to further thought. However, he succeeded in cutting C short in his account of the use of a
plastic skin as a means of spreading weight on the surface of the
water, and his bouts of analysis throughout the session would

probably have been more useful if saved until all ideas had been expressed. And his derision of C's idea for producing an undulating motion might have silenced a less self-sustaining person than C appeared to be.

In reporting this session it must be added that quite a lot of editing has been necessary. Lacing all the recorded narrative together was much that was irrelevant, much 'noise'. This has been filtered out to highlight the significant parts. Coupled with the words were thumbnail sketches on the blackboard offering further, unheeded opportunities for development. And gestures, voice inflections – confidence, uncertainty, scorn – eye-catching and avoiding, laughter, spontaneous at times, but mainly self-conscious. All the tell-tale non-verbal behaviour was there, having an effect at least as great as the verbal. Even so, in one session of about two hours, and using far less than the total energy and abilities shared between them, a group of five young men had come up with some interesting observations on the problem of 'walking on water'. They learned something too about their own behaviour, they agreed, when an observer offered comments on it for discussion at the end. But this was an isolated exercise for the students and, interested as they seemed to be at the time, not one of them checked any of the statements made, or went away to put their ideas to the test. The gap between being creative and being innovative for this group was never bridged.

Compare the performance of the five students with a group of four people, colleagues of long standing but of different backgrounds. Their association had resulted in a mutual respect for each other's ability and an openness and trust between them such that they could be spontaneous in expressing their thoughts without fear of ridicule, yet knowing that each idea would be ruthlessly analysed when the time was right to do so.

Since in this case the group are pursuing the innovation beyond the point we are about to observe, it is presented in a disguised form.

OBSERVATIONS

A Are we all agreed, then, that this part of the problem is

Only part of the problem is presented here and a lot of time how to reproduce words and phrases in foreign scripts on the address labels without the use of transfers or stencils?

had been spent deciding exactly what the problem was before attempting to find solutions.

B My suggestion is that instead of having to transfer a letter from one part to another – take it off here and put it on there – or stencil it by moving the template, we should do as you half suggested before, C. If the label was light sensitive, you could transfer the letter by photography. You would have a sheet with the letters on and move your selector over them – a sort of magic eye thing . . . That wouldn't be terribly expensive . . .

B has picked up an idea thrown up by C and is trying to develop it.

A No . . . well, that's the Xerox type process, I think. If the label you were transferring the symbol to was underneath . . . Imagine this . . . Suppose we have a standard-size label, we could have some sort of simple framework which went over it, and if we had a machine into which we could fit some gadget which had a master craftsman-made image, we could project that image using our guide lines on the

A is taking up B's contribution and suggesting an alternative form . . .

label in the frame. The image could be made permanent . . .

C It would be like using a Xerox a square centimetre at a time . . .

. . . which is supported by C.

D Polaroid cameras. There's instant reproduction.

D contributes something he sees as analogous, but it isn't developed.

A Just taking that a stage further. Think of secret writing. You've got a piece of paper and you sensitize the paper with one chemical which is invisible. You then expose it to another chemical and it comes up. Now if you could do that with this . . .

A seems quite willing to combine the ideas put forward without pushing his own particular suggestions too hard.

D If you had the whole alphabet impressed over the whole of the area you would only need twenty-six different symbols – or whatever the number the language required.

B All right, but think about that combined with my idea. Suppose you have got a label which becomes light sensitive when you roll some chemical over it, you can project your image on it, run your roller over it where the image is and the image would be retained. Then you could move your image-producing gadget to the next space and repeat the process.

OBSERVATIONS

D It has got to be a process
that doesn't react while you
are mucking about getting
set up, but is like a photographic system.

C You wouldn't have to fix the
image every time though –
just run your roller over the
lot when you had finished,
provided you could still see
the image you had left.

A Look, what we want is a little
light pen here – like those
little electric torches the
kids had which projected a
silhouette of Batman on to
the wall – with a sort of
selector thing that enables
you to select your symbol,
play it on the label, and press
a button.

B That's right. And you have
it in a frame to give constant
distance and to allow you to
position it . . .

A But it still allows you to
move it nearer or further
from the label so that the
image can be varied in size –
just like a photographic en-
larger.

A makes a practical suggestion
which seems to express the
ideas all have put forward in
various ways.

This is a small part of the total discussion but serves to give
the flavour of the whole. Conducted with no established rules but
with each person contributing freely and positively, ideas were
built up between them, so that the final solution was an integration of little increments given by each. A great deal of sketching

clarified the words, which at times were only made coherent by the gestures and pictures accompanying them. A sense of confidence was apparent. Members of this team never seemed to doubt their ability to solve the problem and the confidence they showed in each other's competence and their mutual willingness to continue with the task welded them into a highly effective and creative group.

Both the groups presented here produced plenty of ideas. However, one let many of them leak away while the other conserved them and built one upon another. It is clear that the first group dissipated more of its energy in blocking and criticizing than the second. In the latter the flow of ideas was smoother and more constructive. Instead of slamming doors in each other's face they held them open. Each had his say and was listened to. In contrast, the first group had one member who never opened his mouth, and interventions were not always relevant or particularly helpful.

What has been presented are mere fragments of group behaviour, but they are typical of the ways the two teams conducted themselves. They link well with the findings of serious researchers in the field (for instance, Likert, 1961, and Pelz and Andrews, 1966) who have made wide studies of the working and makeup of effective groups.

All seem to be in general agreement on what makes an effective group:

1. Members have a clear idea of what they are trying to achieve and are not easily diverted from their objective.
2. Individual members have a real interest in the problem and its solution. Their personal objectives are consistent with carrying it through to success.
3. Members make a full contribution according to their ability, and assist each other in drawing out ideas. Co-operation and support is accepted as the way of achieving the best result, since everyone can then adopt the attitude of 'I win, we all win', rather than 'I win, the rest lose'.
4. Though personal competition is small, intellectual challenge is high. Conflict, when present, is recognized and dealt with

openly. It is not considered improper to show personal feelings and for these to be taken into account.

5. Short-term leadership tends to rotate according to the immediate needs of the job, in terms of the skill and knowledge required and the particular people who possess them.

6. Decisions are made by the people who are best informed on the subject. These are not necessarily the most senior present.

Confirmation of the validity of these general statements is provided by several investigators. Hitt (1965) proposes an environment which gives the individual freedom to explore and freedom to make mistakes, but holds him personally accountable for his own actions. Eyring (1959) speaks of the importance of a stimulating environment, including freedom from distractions which deflect attention from the question at issue. The individual should profit from congenial surroundings and stimulating company, Eyring says, and preferably should be completely at peace with the world except for the violent conflicts characterizing the problem engaging his attention. (This view is not shared by Maddi (1965), however, who claims evidence indicating that 'the frustration and torment of need states' does not necessarily inhibit creativity.) Mackworth (1965) places the accent on the social and intellectual environment, which he suggests is of much greater importance than physical surroundings. The need for access to the widest possible range of technical information relative to a problem to give support in what is essentially a risky and uncertain venture is stressed by Carr (1966).

Merely to catalogue these factors is not very helpful in developing the effective innovative group, however. We have to check for their presence in any particular situation and do something to build them in when they are absent.

A simple way of diagnosing the state of health of a group is, as we have said, to observe it over a period of time and note how it behaves. Followed by an honest and non-threatening account of these observations (remembering the rules for effective feedback on page 127) it can have a stimulating effect. Or the group itself can become an active partner in the diagnosis by assessing its performance against a simple checklist of the points listed, drawn up with a scale marking from good to poor. Each member can do his own assessment and then discuss his views with his colleagues. If the whole group, especially its leader, is committed to either process and follows it up with specific actions to improve weak points, then real team-building will ensue. Leave out the action, however, and it will be no more than an interesting mental exercise.

Lastly, on the subject of integrating the group, we should discuss leadership. Over ten years ago Burns and Stalker (1961)

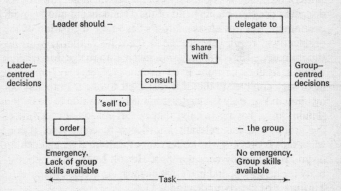

Fig. 10. Leadership styles. (After Tannenbaum and Schmidt)

identified quite different systems of management used in firms, depending upon whether they were well established and static or in a state of change. Management in the latter took the form of information and advice rather than instruction; communication was free, both laterally and vertically, knowledge and experience were made available for solving a problem irrespective of normal boundaries, and individual jobs were adjusted to suit the needs of the occasion rather than to conform to a rigid role. Management of this type was called 'organic', to distinguish it from the 'mechanistic' management appropriate to more static firms. In these, work is organized from the top, often specialized and compartmentalized, and communication is mainly up and down. Structurally the organization is fixed and hierarchical.

Leadership can vary over a wide range according to the situation. A model, Fig. 10, summarizing the suggestions of

Tannenbaum and Schmidt (1958), shows behaviour appropriate
to the needs of the task. At one end of the continuum the leader
makes a decision and orders his subordinates to carry it out: at
the other, he merely sets some limits on the range of decisions and
commits himself to accept the one that the group makes. In
between these extremes he may decide for himself but persuade
his subordinates to accept it; he may consult them before making
a decision; or he may consult and share the decision with them.
Burns' and Stalker's organic style of management lies towards the
delegated decision-making end of the Tannenbaum and Schmidt
continuum. But not always. Most of the time the nature of the
problem will require the leader to share his authority with his
subordinates. They will have as much knowledge for dealing
with it as he does, or more. Even then the problem may sometimes
be of such complexity that it is easier left to one man to sort out
by himself. Probably the leader is in the best position to do it, and
should do so, having ensured that he has consulted everyone in
the group who has relevant knowledge to contribute. Again,
when time is pressing, the leader cannot wait for a group decision
or go in for lengthy consultations. He still carries full responsibility for his group, and in a crisis he must act on his own quickly.
This must be clearly understood.

Having considered the formation of the team and its leadership,
let us now turn to how the leader can give it a sense of direction
and an acceptable discipline for keeping up the pace towards the
achievement of its objective. Features of an effective group are
that it has a clear idea of what it is trying to do and is not easily
diverted from its goal. Its leader has the responsibility to see that
its objectives are understood and the group is able and willing
to achieve them. Participative leadership is often appropriate in
handling innovative work, but the leader will get no medals for
his style; only for his achievements. How can he hope to succeed
when he has to give away much of his direct control to his
subordinates?

The answer lies in what I would call a system of management by
objectives, although many might object to the title. Essentially
what is required is a cycle of operations, a closed loop, in which

actions to be carried out by individuals are clearly understood and properly supported with resources, and completion of these actions is reviewed, consolidated and used as the starting point for another round of activity. Fig. 11 shows the cycle in diagrammatic form.

Members of the team must know first what they are trying to

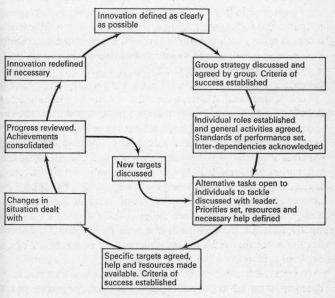

Fig. 11. Management by objective cycle.

achieve. The 'How' may be impossible to define at this stage and the 'How much' next to impossible, but a clear statement of what will be considered a successful end is essential to get people all pointing in the same direction.

Next, the strategy that the group is going to follow must be discussed and agreed. What sort of approach is most appropriate? (In broad terms, because we may have to shift our stance quite a bit as we really get into the problem.) What yardsticks will be used for judging progress?

Then, who is going to do what, again in general terms? What roles are individuals going to have within the team; what will be the essential on-going activities that will be expected of them without further discussion until the end of the innovation, or until a change is agreed? To what minimum standard must these be performed for the satisfactory working of the group? What inter-dependencies will there be and how will these be handled?

Let us mention here that although the leader will be taking the initiative and setting the pace in all this, the process is very much a group affair, with everyone having a share in the discussion and gaining a crisper and deeper knowledge of the project and, it is hoped, increasing his commitment to its successful completion.

Having discussed the strategy, what about the tactics – how does the group start to move forward? Individuals must take on specific tasks within the general framework, be provided with the necessary resources and agree target dates for completion. But despite a sound strategy, excellent planning and diligent work, the innovation team may still fail. It cannot predict certain success. It can only go as far as deciding upon and doing what appear to be the most promising things, and doing them to the best of its ability. By so doing it may then achieve its objective, or it may not. Really all that it has control over is what its individual members do, not what they achieve, and this must be remembered when progress is reviewed.

If a person has undertaken to make a prototype of a machine based on some new concept, his performance can be assessed with justice only on the standard of workmanship displayed, his economy in time and material, and so on. If it is the embodiment of a brand-new idea he cannot be held responsible for its success or failure at this stage. Of course, on review lessons will be learned about the general strategy and individual contributions. By following this cycle, the leader can exert his influence while encouraging participation and a feeling of real ownership of the problem among his team. Recycling should follow a spiral towards ultimate success, with the leader introducing corrective action throughout the sequence, particularly at each review stage (Fig. 12), at which it is asked:

Where are we right now?
Where do we want to be?
Are we still going in the right direction?
What does 'success' look like now?
How are we performing in our present activities?
What should be our next move?

In case this should be considered too easy, let us add the necessary corrective. Throughout the life of a project, the leader

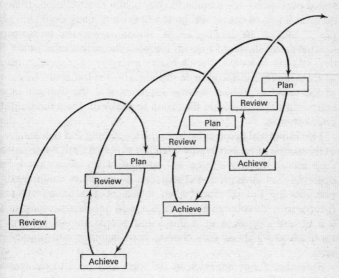

Fig. 12. The innovation spiral.

has continually to ask himself the questions: is it still worthwhile carrying on? do the ultimate benefits together with continuing uncertainty of achieving them justify further efforts? Some sort of regular cost-benefit approach is essential. He must take a wide view of this, naturally: there are other benefits than direct financial profit – prestige, technological leadership and knowledge, advanced skills, social improvements, etc. – but, unless he is careful, there can come a time when the project becomes an end in itself, when completion is the goal instead of intrinsic worth, or when so much money and effort has been spent that to kill it could mean professional suicide for some who have been identified with it.

It is inevitable that the group's style of working will change as the innovation progresses – remember the changing nature of the sequence illustrated in Fig. 8 (page 74) and the corresponding attributes which must be shown within the group to deal with it. Fig. 8 is shown as a simple progression from the original vaguely stated problem to the hammering out of the final solution. It is no such thing, of course. Progress will involve many dead ends, many 'back to the drawing board' situations, and will be more like the spiral shown in Fig. 12. Showing the sequence as linear does allow us to indicate the alternate convergence and divergence in thinking that must occur in dealing with the different phases of the creative problem-solving sequence, and the changes in behaviour required within the group to deal with these differing circumstances.

Two important points arise from this slackening and tightening of the mental reins. Firstly, the discipline expected from the group must change to suit – there will be times when rules must be observed and divergence curbed; and times when traditional practices are out of place, when timekeeping is unimportant (people with ideas buzzing in their heads do not start working at 9 a.m. and stop dead at 5 p.m.) and people should be free to range as widely as they choose, both mentally and physically.

Secondly, the composition of the team may need to change. Most people can adjust their behaviour to suit the needs of the situation. A few do it superlatively well – the great individual innovators, perhaps. A few just can't do it at all. These are the ideas men, who flit from one novel thought to another and who are great to have around when inspiration is fading, but keep on flitting when things need buttoning up. Others are the stern men whose object in life is to smash every idea on sight. It may be better to bring both types of men into the team to play their part at the appropriate time and then move them on before they become a liability.

Other changes which the group may have to cope with are such things as the following:

1. Priorities may change owing to new legislation or altered standards.
2. New routes to the solution may appear through external developments and innovations, or the route being developed may be blocked by a competitor reaching the solution first and protecting himself by patents.
3. Time pressures may change owing to competitors' activities in the same area.
4. The need for the innovation may alter owing to some new external factor.

In all the cases cited, the group must react quickly if it is to cope effectively. It can prepare in a limited way by considering each as an alternative future and making a contingency plan to deal with it. Starting with a possible future situation – say, the initially chosen route being blocked by a competitor's patent and an alternative route successfully developed – it might be possible to work backwards from the alternative situation to where the group is now, thus identifying steps to bridge the gap.

We can now go a step further than Figs. 11 and 12 took us, and by adding the possible shapes of things to come, arrive at Fig. 13.

We spoke of 'strategies' for achieving these alternative futures. 'Plans' would be too definitive. After all, we are dealing with an innovation and we don't know the exact route to our original goal, never mind possible alternatives. What we are doing is to keep a broad view of possibilities and an up-to-date checklist of options still open as we progress towards our chosen goal.

Here is an example. A group of development engineers had to develop a way of measuring the efficiency of a chemical reaction which consisted essentially of heating a raw material in a gas furnace. A lot of dust was generated in the process. The temperature in the burner was much higher than could be tolerated by any proprietary flue gas analysis instrument which might normally be used to gauge the composition of the outgoing gases, and from which could be deduced the efficiency of the whole process. Several alternatives were open to them, each having some chance

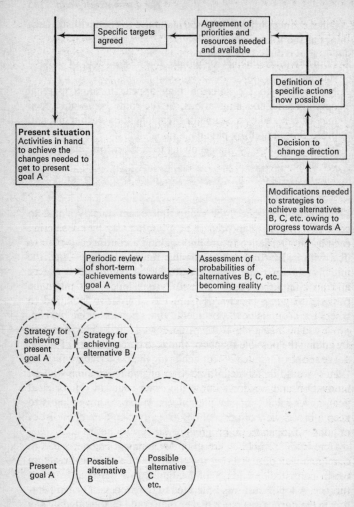

Fig. 13. Alternative future goals.

of success though at different levels of confidence. Time was a crucial factor.

Weighing up the situation, the group decided to pursue the path requiring least innovation but most chance of success: to analyse the flue gas in the discharge chimney, where it had had time to drop in temperature, but had also been diluted with a lot of air which leaked into the system up to that point. Dust remained a problem and the element of innovation really amounted to no more than making the gases dust free.

While pursuing this problem, however, the group took some time to list all the other possible solutions to the more basic problem of burner efficiency. Several came to mind: temperature of the chemical charge itself at the end of the cycle; colour of the flames above the charge during different phases of the heating; certain properties of the dust in the flue gas; and so on. All were considered, and strategies were agreed for tackling each one. These strategies were modified as progress was made on the chosen method of solution: some were discarded because there would be insufficient time left to develop them, but the rest were kept going. In fact, difficulties encountered along the chosen route increased the relative attractiveness of one of the alternatives and a compromise between the two finally emerged as the solution – a compromise that turned out, in fact, to be a better solution than the original.

This is one way of dealing with change, then. Anticipate it, and be ready with an answer. This means spending time on technical 'insurance policies': review meetings have to be held and forward plans made – anathemas to hard-pressed people who just want to get on with the job, and admittedly a waste of time if they are not done properly. But done realistically, against a hard-headed criterion of time-effectiveness, they prove their worth in keeping the group on target with its present task, and are invaluable for providing a signpost when the chosen road peters out.

A word, too, about the attitudes of individual members of the group in times of change. At such points success is governed more than ever by individual goodwill and readiness to adapt mentally (and emotionally) to a change in direction. An organization has a 'psychological contract' with its members as well as a legal one in terms of their commitment to its aims and the depth to which they are prepared to be involved intellectually, emotionally and morally in the enterprise. If it is asking for total commitment, it must be prepared to give genuine reward in return in terms of opportunities for responsibility, autonomy, challenging work and psychological growth.

This is in keeping with the teaching of McGregor (1960), Herzberg (1959), Maslow (1954) and all the others who stress that there is more to work than its physical and intellectual content, and more to reward than the carrot and the stick. Attention to the content of the job – enriching it by creating opportunities for taking on more demanding work and by giving greater personal control – has a beneficial effect on performance and the sheer satisfaction of doing it, according to Herzberg and, more recently, Paul, Robertson and Herzberg (1969).

Others put similar views but in a wider context. E. P. Smith (1969), for instance, in describing the Action Centred Leadership courses run by the Industrial Society, defines three basic needs for effective group work: it must be getting the required results; it must be working well together as a team; and each member must be playing his maximum part. Attention to any one need at the continuing expense of one or both of the others will lead to a reduction in performance, and successful leadership is careful to preserve a reasonable running balance between all three.

One final point before leaving the subject of adjusting to change is the need for keeping people up to date with their technical knowledge and for developing their skills as managers and leaders or effective colleagues in highly complex and demanding situations. Once again this is time-consuming and reduces the immediate energy available for the job in hand. But change does absorb energy in coping with it and unless this is allowed for in on-going plans the problems we thought were going to confront us may turn out not to be the ones that are there in fact, or that the ones that are there are beyond our capabilities.

Finally, let us consider how the group can maintain healthy relationships with the rest of the organization. We have looked at the forces acting on a group from outside: company policy, the esteem in which the work of the group is held, and so on. The group exerts its influence outwards as well. It is a two-way effect. Success by the group influences the rest of the organization and may be reflected in a more supportive and benevolent attitude towards it. Failure, or too much success accompanied by smugness, may provoke a more mixed response. A group's sense of identity increases as it becomes more effective. Pride in achievement leads it to become competitive towards other groups, particularly those working in a similar area. Hostility may follow, nourished by ignorance or distortion of what the other groups are doing due to an increasing gap in communication and a wish to see itself in the most favourable light. A win-or-lose situation can arise in which co-operation on a shared problem is out of the question and each group goes its own way with the attitude of 'winner takes all'; competing for resources, withholding information and generally working towards success for the group rather than the total organization. This isn't entirely bad, of course. It can sharpen group performance and increase internal cohesion. But it can also reduce overall organizational effectiveness, waste energy in duplicated or antagonistic work and lead to departmental fragmentation.

It may be too idealistic to expect 'establishment' groups and innovative groups (whose particular task is to challenge the established system and change it in some way) to adopt a co-operative approach when most of their experience has been competitive. It can be done if the significant people in the organization – the ones with 'leverage' or power – want it to happen, and pay attention to such things as:

1. Promoting a 'systems' view of the situation; stressing the overall goals of the organization and how each section plays its part in an integrated effort; and rewarding group and individual behaviour which contributes to the total effectiveness of the organization.

2. Encouraging 'teach-ins' between groups to improve the passage of information and to bring their respective members together for discussion on shared problems. If such meetings can develop into joint planning situations so much the better, especially if they end with the groups parting with quite specific and mutually agreed actions to be taken by each side.

3. Arranging for interchange of people between the groups to promote increasing knowledge of the work and problems on both sides.

4. When, because of too much hostility, a straightforward sharing of knowledge and perceptions of each other cannot bring groups together, arranging a 'negotiation meeting' when some direct bargaining can take place without any change in attitudes between them. This method, developed by the American psychologist Roger Harrison, can lead to important changes on each side, resulting in mutual advantage and a more mature attitude towards each other. Briefly, each group lists the things it would like the other to do or not to do, or do more of or less of. These lists are clarified by straight questions and answers. Each group then decides amongst its members what it is prepared to do, what it will not do, and what it is prepared to negotiate. Coming together again, the groups discuss their demands and what they have to offer and finally agree changes on a *quid pro quo* basis. Negotiations carried on in this open way make for clarity of expression and precise statements of what is agreed to be done afterwards.

7 Some Acknowledged British Innovators

We now turn to consider five of the country's most distinguished innovators. By examining their backgrounds and noting their attitudes and opinions we get a glimpse of their personalities and working style, and the environment in which they have achieved their successes. Some comparison may then be possible between what suits them and what is helpful for the less gifted individuals, the majority, with whom we have been most concerned in this book.

All five men are acknowledged leaders in their own field: Barnes Wallis in aviation, John Baker in structures, Frank Whittle in jet engines, Alastair Pilkington in glass-making and Alex Moulton in vehicle suspension and bicycle design. There are others still alive in this country whose claim to consideration is as high as those included here; they are excluded only because they were not available for interview. Those that are considered may be representative of the rest, or they may not, and a note of caution is not out of place here. Only the most tentative conclusions can be drawn from the superficial life histories of five men, however eminent they may be, and however enticing it may be to extrapolate the findings. Opinions of colleagues, subordinates and friends, for instance, had they been obtained, might have modified the following accounts.

Let us look at these five men in turn.

In a lifetime beginning well before the Wright brothers achieved sustained flight, Barnes Wallis has made notable contributions at every stage of the emerging history of aviation. In chronological order his designs include:

Seven airships, including the successful R100, and the world's first airship mooring mast.

The Wellesley and Wellington bombers and the geodetic form of construction which allowed much of the airframe to be shot away without losing its rigidity.

The Swallow variable-geometry aeroplane incorporating pivoting wings to give a delta shape for low drag at high speeds and outspread wings for stability at low speeds, and designed (in 1957) to fly at the speed Concorde has only recently achieved.

A hypersonic aeroplane flying at a height of twenty-five miles and able to travel from Britain to Australia in under four hours.

An airship a thousand feet long for transporting natural gas from the Sahara to customers anywhere in the world.

His wholly wartime contributions are no less notable:

The bouncing bomb used in the 'dam-busting' raids during the Second World War, with its novel back spin which enabled it to skim across the surface of the water until it struck the dam wall, when it ran down to explode against the face with devastating effect.

Tallboy, a 12,000-pounder bomb with which the famous 617 Squadron of the R.A.F. sank the Tirpitz and blasted rocket-launching sites and U-boat pens.

Grand Slam, a ten-tonner, whose earthquake effect destroyed bridges and the vital Bielefeld viaduct as the allies advanced through Europe in the last months of the war.

And lastly his 'miscellaneous' designs alone would classify him as a highly productive innovator:

Contributions to the design of a 200-ft radio telescope in Australia.

A flat-sided cargo-carrying submarine, capable of travelling at 30 knots at great depths.

Lighter leg irons for polio victims.

Barnes Neville Wallis was born in 1887, son of a doctor practising in south-east London, and was educated at Christ's Hospital. He left school at sixteen, served a marine engineering apprenticeship and on completion became a draughtsman. During his apprenticeship he attended night school and passed the usual technical examinations, whose standards in his estimation were far below those expected today. Such was his ability, however, that at the end of the First World War when, as an ex-serviceman, he was allowed to shorten the normal academic course, he took his first degree at London University in five months.

Recalling his early days, Barnes Wallis puts great importance on the method of teaching science at Christ's Hospital. In his own words: 'I happened to have had the immense fortune of being at Christ's Hospital just at the time when a very great educationist, and also a great chemist, the late Professor Edward Armstrong, was advocating what he called his heuristic method of education. The Science School at Christ's Hospital was run by a man called Brown, a great disciple of Armstrong's, and we were taught absolutely nothing. You were led up to see what problem existed and Brown would say, "Well, here is a magnificent laboratory, full of fine balances, chemicals and everything you want. Find out why this thing happened."' The laboratories at Christ's were immense and apparatus could be left undisturbed for long periods to suit the boys' needs.

One result of this type of learning was that at the age of sixteen, when his father suggested he should sit the London matriculation examination, he failed. His school, which did not recognize any external examinations whatever, had not equipped him in this direction. 'I knew nothing, except how to think,' he says, 'how to grapple with a problem and then go on grappling with it until you had solved it.'

The attitude learned then clearly became imprinted for life. He claims never to have had a flash of inspiration: '. . . it doesn't work that way with me. Things never come in a flash. A solution comes as a result of months, even years of very heavy work. It is a slow grinding towards the solution, a striving towards the end.' And: 'One never invents or thinks of anything unless you are obsessed by the necessity for that thing to be done. The problem must come first. Then you need to become completely immersed in it, to live with it day and night . . . In a way you might liken a finished product to a Beethoven Sonata. Beethoven spent months, or years polishing his work. He didn't just write down the scores we see. It had to be worked upon and developed, and created over a period of time.'

Barnes Wallis is an autocrat. Not for him design by committee, never a member of a team of equals. Was he unusual in this sense? 'No great development or invention is ever made by a committee. It is always the work of an individual. Nothing makes me more furious than this modern tendency that everybody should have exactly the same amount of property, everybody should have the same income, the same awards. Everything has to be done by a committee of this or that. This way you achieve nothing!'

Did he also mean that discussing a problem with his peers in the intellectual or technological sense would not stimulate him, would not give him ideas? 'No, if I wanted the answer to a question for which I could not do the mathematics I would go to someone who could. I found that I couldn't do the mathematics on how we could run a ball in a rough open sea for two and a half miles. When I found that I couldn't do such mathematics, I went to Sir Geoffrey Taylor and said "Can you give me any solution to the mathematics of pressure development under that ball?" To that extent I would ask for advice and help . . . never a contribution to a solution: really only an explanation of the effects you would get . . . Good design is entirely a matter of one single brain.'

Had he never worked on a problem with anybody else – except when they were in a subordinate position, carrying out his instructions? 'No.' But there were people not connected with the technicalities of his problems who gave invaluable support by opening doors in important places; people who had faith in him and championed his ideas. Lord Tedder, then an Air Vice Marshal, was an invaluable ally in bringing the ten-ton bomb and the earthquake principle to the attention of the people who mattered in Whitehall. Mutt Summers, chief test pilot for Vickers, used his personal friendship with Bomber Harris to ease the situation at the crucial moment when Wallis was trying to get the use of a Lancaster to test his bomb. And Sir Thomas Merton, the physicist, who was a member of the Supply Ministry's inventions tribunal, gave his support at a critical time when the dams' project was almost dropped. Merton arranged for Wallis to go before the tribunal to describe his scheme, adding simply, as Wallis explained idea after idea, that he had never known him to make a mistake. The project was sanctioned.

These people and others helped Barnes Wallis, but it was his own determination, his obsession with a problem once he had recognized it as worthwhile, that really carried him through. Indeed he claims that nothing is more valuable than opposition: 'I think that the more opposition you meet with the harder you will work and the more things you will think of.' His description of engineering design and invention given at the age of eighty-three is forthright and simple. 'It is largely a matter of experience, not of knowledge. Often I can't solve a differential equation. I can go to a young university student who will solve it for me, but he would not be able to design the thing which I have conceived after long years of experience. And you must also have lived long enough in the world to be obsessed with the idea that mankind needs some new type of thing. You go on thinking and thinking until some concept forms slowly and gradually in your mind. And then your background of experience enables you to put it into effect, whereas a young man has not got that background of experience, nor has he got the knowledge of the world which will give him the necessary drive and obsession to put a new thing in. And I can tell you it wants a bit of drive . . .'

A man whose claim to be an innovator is secure though his association with industry has been little more than academic at any time is John Baker, until six years ago Head of the Department of Engineering, Cambridge University. His work has had a major effect on the structural industry through his innovations in design procedure, which have been applied with success to such diverse structures as air-raid shelters, ships' fenders and transportable containers.

John Baker was born in 1901 in Wallasey, Cheshire, the son of a successful businessman turned artist. He had a public school education at Rossall and went on to Cambridge, where he was awarded an open scholarship and graduated with first-class honours in 1923. Finding himself unemployed with no prospect of a job in industry because of the economic situation, he took a job with the Aeronautical Research Committee, though in fact research as a career had never previously occurred to him. 'I was brought up thinking everything was known. There was a colossal lot to learn [at Cambridge] but we were dealing with fundamentals there that would give us the key to everything. The idea of going and finding new knowledge was quite foreign to me . . . I didn't think that there were worlds to conquer in the scientific or innovative sense. I thought there were only industrial worlds to conquer. Our training had led us much more to management, albeit technical management, and I saw myself running a big industry. I had no doubt about my ability to do that . . .'

His job with the Aeronautical Research Committee was proportioning members for the framework of the ill-fated airship R101, but he found the work so boring that he soon left to become an assistant lecturer at Cardiff. Two years later he took the job of Technical Officer to the Steel Structures Research Committee, a collaborative venture between the government and the steel industry. During this period he made his first successful innovation, a gauge for measuring the strains in buildings. It was a case of necessity being the mother of invention, for if he had not succeeded the whole project would have been closed.

In 1933 Baker became Professor of Civil Engineering at Bristol University, where, in conjunction with a colleague, he developed a torque control spanner for use on high-tensile bolts which were being introduced as an alternative to rivets, which even in those days were objected to because of the noise in securing them. Unfortunately the use of high-tensile bolts was ignored by the British steel industry and it was left to the Americans to take it up.

In his work for the steel industry he used the simple and practical approach of taking a real object – a multi-storey building perhaps – and finding how it behaved in reality. When studying how a building collapsed he devised simple tests to find out how the structure actually failed and calculated the accuracy with which its collapse could be foretold. When in 1939 he became a Scientific Adviser in the Ministry of Home Security with an interest in air-raid shelters, he put his experience to good use. Many of the air-raid shelters of the day were quite useless, their walls being so brittle that a bomb falling near by caused them to collapse and the roof to fall onto the occupants. Baker realized that the solution lay in making the walls capable of absorbing energy without shattering and this could be achieved quite simply by reinforcing them with steel rods at nine-inch intervals running vertically and across the roof like so many goalposts. Reinforced in this way shelters could safely withstand a near miss. True, they leapt as high as six feet in the air under such an impact, but so also did the occupants.

Baker used the principle of absorbing energy by allowing a controlled deformation of a structure in his design for the 'Morrison' shelter, which was shaped like a table and intended for indoor use. He had a hard struggle to get it accepted, particularly after a remark made by Winston Churchill to the then Home Secretary, Herbert Morrison, to the effect: 'You must do something for the people. Put something in the houses – something like this,' and Churchill drew an inverted U-shape. This shape was immediately acceptable to the official mind, despite the impracticability of mass-producing it; while Baker's design was opposed.

In 1943 he returned to Cambridge and built up a team to develop a completely new approach to structural design. This has revolutionized the structural steel industry, reducing not only design office effort but the cost of building frames by as much as a third. Based on his concepts for absorbing energy through structural deformation, he designed his 'Cambridge fender' for ships berthing against a jetty or wharf structure, and a container for the fast-growing container industry which cheapened production costs by 30 per cent. Another innovative idea was a collapsible cellular platform for edging aircraft runways, strong enough to bear the weight of fire engines and other vehicles but designed to collapse under the weight of an aircraft and arrest its motion if it taxied off course. Motorways and the absorption of energy in motor car crashes provided a special interest, but no one has put the principles to the test, except a number of Baker's own team who designed a collapsible lamp post.

At over seventy John Baker is in no way disgruntled about the tardiness with which his theories have been applied in practice.

He excuses industry for its unwillingness to come to him with a modest: 'One needs some other gift. There is certainly something lacking in me that doesn't bring people to me . . . Mind you, I was rather rude to the steel industry for about twenty years when they wouldn't see what seemed to me to be the obvious . . . I have no complaints now over the plastic design of building structures. The struggle was long but the method is now accepted world-wide. It hasn't brought much financial reward to me but that was due partly to the particular industry, and partly because I was a mug. My generation was brought up to think that it was immoral to patent, and I didn't, at least until I retired. It was always my feeling that I was the servant of the steel industry and of the community. But undoubtedly if I had patented some fiddling 'plastic joint' early on progress would have been much quicker, because one part of the industry would have taken it up and another would have broken in six months later with something better. And so it would have gone on.

'I don't think I invent at all,' he says. 'I deduce and apply scientific principles. Everything I have done has sprung from the discovery of the value of plastic deformation. I don't think I have ever had a "bright idea" in my life. All my achievements have been the result of many months of heavy development work. Perhaps the only revelation I have experienced occurred when I saw how a fixed-base portal frame would collapse when it became in effect a hinged mechanism. We were stuck for months and months on this, but once it was solved it was difficult to think back to where the blockage had been. But I do believe this was a team "Eureka". There were three or four of us sweating our guts out, thinking, arguing, talking, and we were in a group when it came to us.

'I'm a great believer in team work . . . and the build-up of my team has been most important to me . . . A great deal of my work has really been the achievement of a team. The basic ideas were mine. But during the war, especially, we got several bright people sitting around a table, as it were, with all the ordinary petty restrictions removed and everyone openly giving their views . . . And the amount of original design work we did in four years was staggering . . .

'I have spent half of my life trying to make a branch of the construction industry more efficient. And now I am continuing this with a firm, I.D.C., which does the whole job. Being both designers and builders we have broken through the traditional barrier dividing design from construction, the cause of much frustration, strife and inefficiency. Working in this completely integrated team is as thrilling as any experience I have ever had. What more could any man ask for?'

Frank Whittle has always made it quite clear that the principle of the gas turbine had been recognized long before his time, as had the problems preventing its use in practice. His contribution was to solve these problems. The concept of the jet engine was not his creation, but the jet engine that first left the ground in the Gloster/Whittle E28/39 on 8 April 1941 was his innovation.

It had a long gestation period, beginning in 1928, when, as a Flight Cadet at the Royal Air Force College, Cranwell, he wrote a thesis on 'Future Developments in Aircraft Design'. In it he speculated on the possibility of high speeds at great heights; speeds of 500 miles per hour, when the top speed achieved at the time was about 150 miles per hour. To get such a speed at a height where air resistance would be sufficiently low would need something different from the conventional piston engine driving a propeller: something like a rocket or a gas turbine . . .

Whittle, the first son of a moderately successful mechanic, was born in 1907 in Coventry. His parents had moved earlier from Lancashire, where his father had begun work at the age of eleven in a cotton mill. When Frank was nine his parents moved again, this time to Leamington Spa. There his father bought a small business with an imposing name, the Leamington Valve and Piston Ring Company. For a time he was practically on his own and at the age of ten Frank gained his first experience of drilling valve stems and operating a lathe. He was rewarded for his efforts on a piecework basis.

In his autobiography, *Jet: The Story of a Pioneer*, Whittle continues the story of his life – his early school days at local council schools, his unexpected success at gaining a scholarship to a secondary school, his very indifferent scholastic performance (he didn't like homework) and his growing interest in aircraft engineering, fed by an avid reading in the Leamington Spa reference library. At the age of fifteen he tried to join the R.A.F. as an aircraft apprentice but failed the medical examination because he was too short. Although he soon put on the necessary inches his second attempt to join was equally unsuccessful; once rejected there was no second chance. In the end he had to cheat to get in by pretending that he had never applied before.

After completing a three-year apprenticeship, he was awarded a cadetship at the R.A.F. college. Again he was unfortunate at first. Only five cadetships were awarded and he passed out sixth. But one of the successful ones failed his medical and Whittle took his place. In his fourth term as a flight cadet he wrote his thesis, the one which predicted his future obsession.

The jet-propulsion gas turbine was not his only innovation, however. For four years he was a general duties officer, flying, acting as a flying instructor, stunt pilot and floatplane test pilot, and being launched from experimental catapults. He also found time to invent an improved form of centrifugal compressor, a single-fluke anchor, a scheme for simplifying the handling gear of floatplanes, a means of representing the field of fire from the various gun positions of a flying boat on a single diagram, an enclosed gun turret, an improved bomb hoist for aircraft mounted on catapults, and an entirely new type of catapult. None of the inventions got anywhere. He was commended for his initiative in preparing the field-of-fire diagrams and the rest of his proposals were forgotten. A later invention, his 'flying bolas', which was similar to the South American bolas (three weights joined by ropes tied together in a Y formation), was accepted for trials, but he never found out what happened to it.

His interest in technical matters did not go unnoticed, however. He was recommended for a two-year officers' engineering course and completed it in eighteen months. Then came another of his near near-misses. It had been the practice for the Air Ministry to select one or two officers from the officers' engineering course to attend Cambridge University to take the Mechanical Science Tripos. But the practice had been discontinued shortly before his time. Once again he was lucky, or rather his ability was recognized, and he was allowed to go to Cambridge as an exceptional case. He obtained a First in his Tripos examination in 1936 – in two years instead of the customary three.

All this time he had been thinking of his turbo-jet engine. A fellow officer supported him and gave practical help in drafting the complete specification for his patent, and in making contact with commercial firms. Nothing came of the latter, however. There was no enthusiasm for a development which it was estimated might cost £60,000 – right in the middle of the slump – and made by an unqualified serving officer of twenty-three! 'Whittle's Flaming Touch-hole' became a joke and, in 1935, when his 1930 patent became due for renewal at a fee of £5, he allowed it to lapse. Later, while still at Cambridge, he formed Power Jets Ltd with two former R.A.F. officers to develop his idea, acting himself as Honorary Chief Engineer and Engineering Consultant.

By 1939 the Air Ministry had concluded that Whittle's jet engine might become a practical means of powering an aircraft, and Power Jets were contracted to produce an engine for an experimental aeroplane to be manufactured by the Gloster Aircraft Company. This engine, designated 'W1X', first took to the air on 8 April 1941, when the test pilot did three short hops of 200–300 yards during taxying trials. The first official test flight was five weeks later, on 15 May, very appropriately at Cranwell, where, thirteen years before, Cadet Whittle had written his prophetic thesis on 'Future Developments in Aircraft Design'. By this flight it might be said that Power Jets had transformed the jet engines from a dream into a reality, and had laid the cornerstone of a new industry in this country – and in the United States too, for details of the engine were passed on to the General Electric Company of America and they began intensive development in their works at Lynn, Massachusetts. The 'W1X' engine was sent to them for experience and is now in the Smithsonian Institution.

(In his lecture to the Institution of Mechanical Engineers, Whittle discussed the parallel developments of the jet engine in Germany. The Germans certainly had a type of jet-propelled plane, the Heinkel He 178, which was recorded as having flown for ten minutes nearly two years before the Gloster/Whittle E28/39. But it was subsequently abandoned, and the jet engine which powered the Me 262 in operation before the end of the war did not fly until after Whittle's W1. They had this engine in operation before the British had theirs, but it was put into operation before it had been developed properly and was technically far behind the British engine.)

Power Jets lasted for only ten years and never employed more than 1,400 people at any time. Without friends, Whittle and his company would not have survived for as long as they did. Sir Henry Tizard, Chairman of the Aeronautical Research Committee, was especially helpful. He gave support when it was really needed: 'I have a very high opinion of Flight Lieutenant Whittle,' he wrote in 1937, when Power Jets were in financial difficulty. 'He has the ability and energy and enthusiasm for work of this nature. He also has an intimate knowledge of practical conditions – this combination of qualities is rare and deserves the utmost encouragement. I sincerely hope he will get the necessary finance because I think you will have to make up your mind that a large expenditure will be necessary before final success is reached.'

Lord Tedder – Air Vice Marshal Tedder in those days – was another friend. After a visit in 1940 to see the first engine on test he wrote to Whittle to say how glad he was to have an opportunity of seeing his 'child' in action, and having seen it he felt even more than before that it was up to him to do all he could to help it forward.

Whittle resigned from Power Jets in 1946 and became Technical Adviser on Engine Design and Production to the Controller of Supplies (Air). In 1948 he was awarded £100,000 free of tax and a few weeks later was retired from the Royal Air Force with the rank of Air Commodore. He received a knighthood in the same year. His technical achievement was recognized nationally and internationally by awards, medals and honorary doctorates.

After that he worked as an engineer and consultant to a number of firms and formed a company with Bristol Siddeley Engines to develop a turbo drill for drilling boreholes for oil and natural gas.

Now he is virtually retired but, although he claims to have done no engineering work for some time, his study still has a drawing board in it and a blackboard with calculations – an equation representing a complete gas-turbine cycle, for instance. 'I keep a thing like that on the blackboard maybe for weeks,' he explained, 'and keep coming back to it to see whether I can simplify it . . . If I could simplify the gas-turbine cycle even further, you could do quicker comparisons – for instance if you're going to design a turbo fan and you want to know what is the by-pass ratio for quick cruising conditions, you may have to do several calculations, and the simpler you can make the basic cycle the easier those calculations are to perform . . .'

Although he was Chief Engineer of Power Jets with responsibility for all engineering, and doing most of the basic thinking himself, he gives full credit to the engineers whom he recruited and formed into a team around him. 'I think this job (the jet engine) owes a great deal to the men we picked. We had a marvellous team. They were young, mainly. Four of us were first-class honours Cambridge men, two were Whitworth Scholars, and, I think, about seven others were of equal academic standard. It was a pretty strong team academically. I chose these people personally, in the main by interview and by their background. I judged from the interviews if they would be good practical men as well . . .' An urgent common purpose helped the team to grow, and war-time conditions ('working in a dirty old foundry – people sitting on the stairs because there was nowhere else for them to sit') added to the team spirit.

Regarding himself, Whittle has this to say. 'I have always maintained that my experiences as a pilot were of vital importance to the practical development of the jet engine. To me it was important that when you rammed the throttle wide open the engine should respond. I know what it is like when you come in and you muff your approach and you've got to go round again. You can't afford to have your engine die on you when you open the throttle . . . I always saw myself in the cockpit operating that engine, and what I wanted was just to press a button to start everything. And that is what we got in the end.'

Before discussing the man behind the greatest innovation in the glass industry in modern times, let us take a quick look at the evolution of the techniques in flat glass making from ancient times to the present day. 'Flat' is the significant word here, for the pursuit of flatness combined with cheapness has been the aim of glass makers for years, to satisfy the huge demand for windows throughout the world. Pilkington's own review of the float glass process given to the Royal Society (Pilkington, 1969) gives a convenient guide.

The oldest and most commonly used method was the crown process, in which a disc of molten glass was spun at the end of an iron rod until it reached a diameter of about 4 feet. Only small panes could be cut from a 'crown' of this size because of the thickening at the centre where it had been attached to the iron rod. Sizes greater than those obtainable from a 'crown' were possible with the cylinder process. In this a cylinder of glass was blown, allowed to cool and then split and flattened. Hand blowing by this method produced sheets up to 12 feet by 6 feet. By the start of the twentieth century mechanical blowing increased this size up to about 40 feet by 10 feet. The third development occurred in about 1914, and consisted of drawing a sheet of glass vertically from a bath of molten glass. To prevent 'waisting-in' the edges of the sheet were stiffened by passing them between cooled rollers. Glass made in this way has an unblemished fire-finish because it is allowed to cool down while still suspended out of contact with anything solid. Owing to small differences in viscosity, however, it suffers a certain amount of distortion. Sheet glass made in this way is also relatively cheap, because of the simplicity of the process, but only thin sheet is produced.

To produce thicker, distortion-free sheets required for shop windows, mirrors and, later, motor-car windows, the plate-glass method was developed, involving casting glass on to a table, rolling it into a plate and annealing it before grinding it flat on both sides and giving it a final polish. The process was complicated and very expensive and although improvements were introduced in the shape of a continuous rolling process, later combined with a continuous melting furnace and continuous grinding and polishing, the production of plate glass remained a difficult, costly and rather wasteful process. Glass of extremely high surface quality was produced, however, and this standard would have to be matched by any alternative method. Not only that, but it would have to be cheaper.

In his address to the Royal Society, Pilkington describes his alternative: 'In the float process, a continuous ribbon of glass moves out of the melting furnace and floats along the surface of an enclosed bath of molten tin ... The ribbon is held in a chemically controlled atmosphere at a high enough temperature for long enough time for the irregularities to melt out and for the surface to become flat and parallel. Because the surface of the molten tin is dead flat, the glass also becomes dead flat.

'The ribbon is then cooled down while still advancing across the molten tin until the surfaces are hard enough for it to be taken out of the bath without the rollers marking the bottom surface; so a ribbon is produced with uniform thickness and bright fire polished surfaces without any need for grinding and polishing.'

It sounds so simple. Yet it took seven years and four million pounds before the process could produce float glass which could replace glass made by the plate method. By a fluke, the natural thickness of float glass produced on tin is approximately 6 mm., which was the thickness required by half of the market. The other half wanted thicker and thinner glass. It took another two years to develop a method of stretching the glass from its natural 6 mm. to half that thickness and another three years to perfect a way of arresting the flow of molten glass so that its thickness built up to 5 cm. or more.

Although Alastair Pilkington shares the family name of Britain's premier glass manufacturing company, Lionel Alexander Bethune (Alastair) Pilkington is in fact only a distant relative. He joined Pilkington Brothers because his name was Pilkington, but in a curious way. His father became friendly with Captain Richard Pilkington because of their mutual interest in the family and it was Richard Pilkington who suggested that Alastair might try for a job with the company when he graduated from Cambridge in 1947, after war service, including four years as a prisoner of war.

He tried, and was accepted – an engineer, the son of an engineer and the grandson of an engineer, following his own inclination to carry on the family tradition. Because of his relationship, distant though it was, he was allowed to join Pilkington Brothers as a 'family member'. The company was then still privately owned, and such distinction conferred both privileges and duties upon him. As a family entrant his training and development was planned and very challenging. The rules were simple, but strict; he was expected either to get on to the board or leave the company. In six years he was on the board, by a series of giant steps. Starting as a technical assistant, working in a development team on glass making, and learning about the business from the level of the shop floor (though always known as Mr Alastair), he became production manager and deputy works manager of the company's Doncaster works after two years. Later he returned to St Helens as assistant to the Production Director.

Pilkington Brothers led the world at this time in the simultaneous grinding of both faces of plate glass and he was given the job of commissioning the first Pilkington twin grinder into America. This was a significant experience, he recalls, because for the first time he found that occasionally he hadn't got enough work to fill his time, and he became bored. It was during this time that he began to think about the great reward that was waiting for any firm which could combine the two processes that had run in parallel throughout glass-making history: the inexpensive method for producing poor-quality though nevertheless high-surface-finish glass, and the expensive method for casting and grinding high-quality plate glass. During his time at Doncaster he had been involved in some work involving molten glass and molten metals and was aware of the properties of the two, particularly at their interface. Tin had been one of the metals concerned.

The idea of using the perfectly flat surface presented by molten metal as a means of obtaining an equally flat surface of glass by the simple expedient of floating one on the other came to him when he was helping his wife to wash up. There was no connection between his thoughts and his domestic duties at the time, he recalls, contrary to popular belief.

Returning from America he was told he could pursue this idea. A year later, in 1953, he was put in charge of plate-glass production. This position was ideal for developing his method. He had authority, short lines of communication, resources, men available on the plant and an experimental engineering team under his control. He also had a continuous flow of glass available on which to carry out development work. Even with all these things in his favour the next few years were testing, to say the least. The question of money became more and more severe as development went on. Expenditure went up enormously as they got nearer to production and attained frightening proportions when they reached it. Spending at a rate of about £100,000 a month for no return took courage, particularly for a family concern! Yet neither he nor his fellow directors ever despaired. Even after fourteen months of production making completely unsaleable glass he received full support. He says of this period:

'It was a pretty rugged time. One wondered how long everybody could stand it – not only the people who were working on it but also the people who had to raise the money and approve it. You couldn't go on for eternity doing that. And you had to be absolutely honest about the thing: that you weren't just pigheadedly going on pursuing something that was impossible of attainment.

'The reason we kept going was that every single fault that we met had yielded some time or other to a direct frontal attack on it. But we were incapable of producing glass that was free of all faults at any one time. Sometimes the glass was of unsaleable quality because of a number of different faults at the same time: too much distortion, stuff falling on the top surface, faults on the bottom surface, difficulties of control with the glass snaking along the surface of the bath, and so on. But we hadn't met any fault that had shown itself impossible to get rid of, so we couldn't say that it was an impossible process to bring through to success.

'The other thing that helped to keep us going was the awareness that if we could do it, it was a big thing. It wasn't worth fooling around spending a lot of money on something that, even if it came through, wasn't very important to us. So we were prepared to take greater risks where we had a big reward–effort ratio if we could bring success.

'Our chairman was unwavering in his support for it. I used to

say, jokingly, "Your certainty of success is related to the fact that
you don't know how difficult it is." Right in the middle of our
period of chaos on the production plant he maintained that even
if it failed it would have been worth every penny . . . I'm sure that
each person [on the board] must have had a slightly different view
of the likelihood of success and how long we would go on, but up
to that stage they were absolutely solid in backing it. There was
never a meeting of the board when they said, "We really think
we ought to be stopping soon." This made an enormous
difference.

'I can tell you it is a very complicated process, and to get it
under control was very difficult. It took us many years after
making our first saleable glass to get to the point where we could
say that we had this process pretty well under control.'

During this time he was very much concerned with directing
the practical day-to-day development work. For a period he held
three meetings a day, discussing progress, assessing results and
deciding and planning the next step. He made a point of taking
the manager in charge away from the sound of breaking glass so
that they could talk. Just getting somewhere quiet and away from
the job for a while helped in seeing the problems in better perspective and often led to sounder decisions than those considered
in the turmoil of the production shed. He says:

'The actual battle to keep something going and the effort going
into it was very bad for decision-making. We always tried to hold
our meetings in rooms where it wasn't possible to hear the noise of
breaking glass. We had breaking glass for years on end and it was
a disturbing sound. You felt that you really ought to rush out and
do something – anything – to stop it; whereas what you had to do
was to deal with the immediate problem very quietly and purpose-
fully and identify what question you had to answer and what was
the best way to do it. And then try to imagine what should be the
next move so that you could order the next bit of equipment;
otherwise you might suddenly have the whole pilot plant with
nothing to do because you hadn't got some vital bit ready.'

Alastair Pilkington has a high regard for his development team,
some of whom are still with him. Its manager was a man of great
courage, a very good engineer who had an ability to go straight

into things and do them without any uncertainty. Engineering played a very big part in development. 'We were always building new plants, or modifying them,' he says, 'and this engineer worked very fast, from identifying a need, getting a drawing done and getting a thing made . . . I believe this to be a very important thing in projects like this; if possible to get ahead of what you are trying to do. A very big part of the time was spent in deciding what ironmongery you wanted and then designing and making it. You designed a Mark One, made it and tried it, and then you modified it and started on a Mark Two. And so you went on. Another big thing was the tremendous importance of getting an analysis of your results really quickly and accurately in such a way that you could make good decisions. The thing went on day and night. We never stopped. It was very demanding to do development work on a continuous process and it never let you go to bed without wondering if everything was still going on.

'I feel very strongly about the great need to separate the directing of the project from the managing. In my experience, the projects which have not separated one from the other have nearly all been failures. Managing the hour-to-hour, the day-to-day, even the week-to-week running of a plant is a very demanding job. Directing is asking the right questions: is the team the right sort of team? is it getting support? are the production people getting involved to be sure that they can take over at the right time? are we going to make a profit? and where is the money coming from? It is a terribly dangerous thing to mix these two things up because both will probably be done badly.'

Discussing his personal thinking process, he recalls an occasion during the development of the later process for producing thin ($\frac{1}{8}$ in.) float glass. After turning the problem over and over in his mind, he mentioned it to a colleague, who said, 'I don't know why you don't have two float baths: make the glass in one and then pass it into the other.' The words triggered off a train of thought which resulted in the development of the stretching process requiring operations at two temperatures albeit in the same float bath. His colleague had meant something quite different, but the words had acted as a cue to start his mind working in a new direction.

On trying to solve a problem which demands a creative approach he says: 'I know I need to start as it were with a clean sheet of paper. It's no good my starting off by reading all the literature on the subject. I have to try to get a clear picture of my idea. A definition of success in that area has to be made clear for me before I start ... If I get cluttered up with other people's ideas and other people's definitions of what should be done, this totally confuses me in the first instance. I know I shall have to say, "What is this all about and what would be success? Do I feel clear about what I need to bring into effect?" This is essential for me. I know my best thinking is always done when I can get down quietly and start approaching a problem with an absolutely fresh mind. If I can sweep everything to one side and start in a very elementary way this helps me.'

Aids to creative thinking are not scorned, however, and not only has he tried them himself and found them useful, but he actively encourages his staff to use them. But the essential factor in a company is to get people to believe that they are encouraged to be creative. 'Of everything, I believe this is the most important single thing to get across ... There must be evidence of your sincerity ... And you must get people to believe that they have it in them to be creative; that nobody will make them look a fool when they put an idea forward, and that it won't be difficult to get it tried out in its initial stages.

'I've always wanted to create, and it's a surprise to one that more people don't go around thinking that they can find new and better ways of doing everything. A surprisingly small number of people seem to enjoy the idea of creating new ideas. It isn't the thought of reward that drives creative people along. It's unimaginable that anyone would start thinking about new ideas with the object of getting a reward, because you're very remote from such a thing when you're at the beginning of a new idea. Downstream you have got all the pain of trying to take the thing through and nothing of any importance has ever been achieved without it being very uncomfortable. I imagine that nine out of ten inventors are extremely frustrated human beings, because they don't feel they are close enough to the resources and the decision about the deployment of resources. I was extraordinarily fortunate about this. I must be one of the very few people who have been allowed to take his own idea through and be supported all the way, and I recognize that as a very privileged position.'

In 1848, Alexander Moulton's great grandfather, Stephen Moulton, founded a business in a derelict wool mill for the manufacture of vulcanized rubber under Charles Goodyear's patent. This was the origin of the vulcanized rubber industry in England, the rubber produced being used for capes in the Crimean War and for buffers and draw springs on the railways. Later the family business was merged with Spencers, who were consultants in railway engineering, and the firm of George Spencer, Moulton and Company continued to manufacture rubber in Bradford on Avon until 1956, when it sold out to the neighbouring Avon Rubber Company.

Alexander Moulton was born in 1920, and spent his childhood in Bradford on Avon before going to Marlborough College. In 1937 he became an engineering apprentice with the Sentinel Steam Waggon Company in Shrewsbury because of his early interest in steam for automotive use, and then went up to King's College, Cambridge, to read for the Mechanical Sciences Tripos. During the war he worked on aero engine research at the Bristol Aeroplane Company, where he became Personal Assistant to Sir Roy Fedden, to whom he acknowledges a great debt for his early training.

He displayed an interest in engineering in general at a very early age, recalling that when he was four or five he got a model aeroplane from the estate carpenter. It was made of solid wood and he was chastened when a gardener said that an aeroplane wasn't made like that, but was of wood with canvas stretched over it. This introduction to technical realities in his childhood, he says, led to a lifelong interest. From then on he knew exactly what he wanted to do: to be an engineer and to create new mechanical things.

'I'm in no way interested in maintaining an existing thing. I've never wished to manage a mass-production shop. My concern has been with problems of creation, improvement and design for manufacture. I'm moved by an interest and a curiosity for

technical artefacts and derive a deep satisfaction from understanding the whole nature of a problem and its solution.'

When he was about fourteen and away from home at school he
became interested in developing a steam-driven car. To that end
he scoured the technical literature on the subject and haunted the
Science Museum in London. So that he could get on with the job
when he was ready he got hold of an ancient lathe which he had
sent to school during term time and back home again for his
holidays. He developed some skill in the use of tools by visiting
his friend, the local blacksmith.

He made it all himself, 'hewing it out of the solid, filing and
hacksawing and drilling holes far too large in diameter with a
belly brace, without power in a cold workshop, sometimes until
3 o'clock in the morning . . . I was doing it far too primitively in
an unskilled, unhelped, unequipped way and I got almost a
hatred for doing things in this way.

'You cannot be innovative in engineering unless you have the
means to make and the means to measure. I've seen to it ever
since that time that I'm well equipped. And it's no use being well
equipped if the whole thing is a muddle.'

In 1943 he left the Bristol Aeroplane Company to join the
family firm and in time became Technical Director. He built up a
research department and began his work on rubber suspensions
for vehicles, in 1948 inventing his first suspension unit, the
Flexitor, which consisted of an inner shaft and outer shell with an
annular rubber body bonded in between, after the pioneering
design of Alvin Krotz in the United States.

When the family sold out to the Avon Rubber Company in
1956, Alexander Moulton formed Moulton Developments and,
using the stables of his home as premises, continued his work on
vehicle suspension. Sponsored by the British Motor Corporation
and in close association with their designer, Issigonis, and the
Dunlop Rubber Company, he invented a rubber cone spring in
1951 which was used later on the BMC Mini range. By 1963
some 2·5 million of these units had been manufactured by
Dunlop.

In 1954 he took out a patent for his Hydrolastic suspension
system. As with all profound technological innovations, the idea

is simple in hindsight. All four wheels of the car are independently sprung by means of a combined rubber spring and damper assembly but the pairs of wheels on each side are interconnected front to rear by a hydraulic system. When one front wheel passes over a bump and closes the front suspension, fluid is displaced from the front wheel suspension unit to the rear wheel unit causing it to open and so prevent pitching. In this way the pitch frequency is reduced. When both wheels on one side are deflected together, as when cornering at speed, there is no displacement of fluid from front to rear but the increased fluid pressure in the suspension units deflects the rubber springs and the whole system provides a high degree of stiffness in roll.

In 1962 he formed a second company, Moulton Bicycles Limited, to produce his novel bicycle, on whose design he had been working in parallel with his motor vehicle suspension. He believes it to be a good idea to keep more than one project going at the same time. He explains, 'I'm sure from a creative point of view that it's important to have one or two dissimilar lines of thought to follow. Not too many, but just so that you can rest one groove in the mind and work in another.'

His interest in the bicycle is of long standing. Cycling has always been a particular hobby and the bicycle to him is a delightful machine. When he came to examine a standard machine in a disciplined, rigorous way he found that ergonomically it was excellent; the orthodox posture for the rider was correct and the pedal crank drive could not be bettered. But why were the wheels so large in diameter, giving them so much inertia and making acceleration and manoeuvring difficult? Why was it necessary to have different sizes and shapes for men and women? Why couldn't things be carried on it? and why couldn't it be just more pleasing to ride? He realized that the bicycle of the day had reached a classical form and any change would have to offer a significant evolutionary step to be economically successful. A new bicycle would have to be noticeably more attractive to ride than the conventional one. People must want to ride it in preference to the old model.

Reducing the diameter of the wheels came first, in conjunction with high-pressure tyres. Then the idea of replacing the conventional frame with a monocoque form was considered but was rejected in 1959 because of jointing problems and because the box-like structure transmitted road noise at a quite unacceptable level. This forced a fresh line in thinking, a 'jerk change' to the unique 'F'-frame construction which, combined with novel front and rear rubber suspension, characterized the eventual design.

The whole evolution of the Moulton bicycle is shown in a room converted into a small museum at the hall where Alexander Moulton lives, each model beautifully finished in every detail. 'We have the capability to make immaculate prototypes very quickly,' says its creator. 'I'm absolutely adamant about the quality of our workmanship. We couldn't operate otherwise. We lack nothing in skill, and only size distinguishes us from a full-scale manufacturing concern.'

This was proved quite conclusively, for when no bicycle manufacturer would take up production under licence, Moulton Bicycles went into business in a quite modest workshop erected near the stables on the estate and built 25,000 in the years 1963 to 1966. In 1967 the company sold out to Raleigh Industries Ltd, but today, as Bicycle Consultants Ltd and in association with Raleigh, they are continuing to develop the design which they pioneered in the early 1960s. Currently there are prototypes of the second-generation Moulton bicycle, of yet higher efficiency.

The main activity, however, at Moulton Developments Ltd occupying the one-time bicycle factory is automative suspension research and developments.

A visitor to this tiny firm – it numbers about forty in all – is struck by the tremendous discipline and attention to detail displayed by everyone. In this sense they are influenced by Alexander Moulton himself, who makes no secret of his insistence on these characteristics, or of his complete authority over what should be done. Although the concept of the project and the decision as to the way ahead, step by step, comes from him, he is concerned to make all those working on the project as self-motivating as possible in order to maximize each individual's contribution. He sees his own role as constantly checking the validity of the steps so as to be within the concept – to keep the project on course:

encouraging logical thought and accurate observation all the time. In this he emphasizes the importance of ordered display of data as it evolves from testing, of looking back to fundamentals and of logical discussion.

Moulton is perhaps unusual as an innovator in being concerned for the longer-term future, with depositing truths that have been established by the team in 'Design Bibles' which form a growing diary of learning acquired as the team progresses through its projects. Writing these Design Bibles has become part of the accepted duties and is regarded as a valuable discipline.

It is conceivable that one of the team might come forward with an idea that is completely outside the company's sphere of activity. What then? 'I don't think anyone has, but if someone did and he were really moved to develop it I would encourage him to go elsewhere and do it himself. And I should wish him every success and help him to do it.'

Nearly half of the team are graduates, but their work does not stop at intellectual office work. Ideas and calculations must be translated into drawings, drawings must be made into hardware as soon as possible, so that reality can be tested and analysed. This is the most important part of the development cycle. Moulton's graduates have drawing boards in their offices, but are just as likely to be bending over the job in the workshops as over their ideas on paper.

In its meticulous layout of jobs and its clear display of test results the workshop is another reflection of its owner's attitude towards successful innovation: to produce ideas, put them to the test, observe the results, diagnose the mode of failure by observation, make a modification based on logical deduction and start again. He is dedicated to the orderly display of information, to accurate observation and the forcing of a logical argument. Test results must therefore be shown so that they are both immediately intelligible and comprehensive over the whole series, so that trends are obvious at a glance.

His 'Discourse Room' shows the same dedication to logical evolution. Surrounded by shelves bearing exhibits of all stages in the development of the Hydrolastic system and the newer designs laid out in strict order, attention is brought to the present by a sketching area on the wall for the up-to-the-moment development of ideas. And even this is kept strictly up to date.

'I like a significant amount of time on my own,' he says. 'It's very necessary in creative work to have a considerable amount of time for thinking. I don't get anywhere at all without a lot of thought. During the daytime my time will be spent on executive actions, but I can use my evenings on the preliminary work for my designs or struggling with the decisions I have to make. I am one of those people who believe in doing their thinking first before talking with others. But the value of an orderly discussion to advance the concept can be considerable.'

Now in his early fifties he can contemplate the day when he can devote more time to his estate. But he is quick to add: 'I hope to have an interest in what I'm doing now till my dying day. Obviously as one grows older one's powers get less and the centre of the field must be taken by others. Even so, I would never like to turn my back and be unable to have some little project to take an interest in or satisfy my curiosity on how it was going.'

Creative design, achieving something elegant and aesthetically pleasing which yet stands up to rigorous analysis and test, is his lasting aim. His is a disciplined and logical approach to creativity, each step being controlled in an evolution towards a desired end product. These steps, he says (Moulton, 1965), should be accomplished 'at a fury of speed so that the pressure of creativity is maintained and doubt held at bay'. Then fantasy must be checked against reality.

Aesthetics are a guide to the rightness of the thing, but the discipline of the engineer must assert itself too: 'I think this discipline is to allow yourself to be humbled in the face of evidence that you carefully weigh and carefully consider, all the time rejoicing if the proposition, from wherever it comes, makes the whole gadget better.

'Thinking is a hard cerebral process. It mustn't be imagined that any of these problems are solved without a great deal of thought. You must drain yourself. The thing must be observed in the mind and turned over and over and over again in a three-dimensional sort of way. And when you have gone through this process you can let the computer in the mind, or whatever it is, chunter around while you pick up another problem. You must always be trying to push the thing back into reality, though, rejecting the negative and choosing the best alternative as you go along.'

But creativity is very personal. 'It's my belief that a new technical concept must spring from the creative impulse of an individual, who in turn will show his proclivity for design at an early age: to attempt to design by committee is unfructuous ... The transformation of a new concept into an engineering and production reality depends absolutely – unlike the work of an artist – upon effective collaboration between several groups of men.'

He believes that it has been an advantage to do his work remote from industrial centres and to keep his development team down to a very small number, well served by superb equipment for swift manufacture and testing. By these means, he says, by holding the single objective of the excellence of the end product always in view, false steps can be taken without inhibition and rapidly rectified.

Success has attended the practice of these precepts. Moulton Developments were awarded the Queen's Award to Industry in 1967 for technical innovation in the Hydrolastic car suspension and the Moulton bicycle. Alexander Moulton has been honoured by Design Awards, honorary doctorates and prizes for his personal contributions.

And he is still busy with his innovations in the area of motor-car suspension. His Hydragas suspension system has lately appeared in the new BLMC 'Allegro' car.

Having described the lives, achievements and attitudes of these five men, let us summarize the main features to see if there is any common thread. Table 1 draws together the similarities and individual differences observed.

Although each has reached his particular pinnacle through individual excellence and dedication, none comes from what could be called a deprived background, a reaction to which might be a desire to succeed against all odds. On the contrary, their origins are upper middle class. Their ability to pass through the

TABLE 1: *Five British Innovators: Summary of Personal History and*

Personal Feature	Wallis	Baker
Father's occupation	Doctor	Business man/artist
Education	Public school (Christ's Hospital)	Public school (Rossall School)
Early academic performance	Failed matriculation because education did not prepare for examinations	Open scholarship to Cambridge
Occupation, if any, before university	Apprenticeship and industrial design (25 years)	—
University	London	Cambridge
Practical training	Apprenticeship to ship building	Government research
Approximate age when innovating	R80 Airship – 34 R100 Airship – 43 Wellesley Bomber – 50 Wellington Bomber – 51 Dam-buster bomb – 56 Grand Slam Bomb – 57 Wild Goose Swing Wing Plane – 66 'Swallow' Swing Wing Plane – 72 Cargo Submarine – 84 Supersonic Plane – 84 1000 ft Airship – 84	'Morrison' indoor air-raid shelter – 40 Concept of plastic design – 35–50 Ship's fender – 65 Container – 65
Stimulation for innovations	Mainly military needs	Wartime defence needs Dissatisfaction with irrational design methods
Professional function other than creator	Chief Designer	Professor
Major sources of strife over innovations	The Establishment	Steel industry 'establishment'. Wartime Establishment (over air-raid shelters)

Attitudes

Whittle	Pilkington	Moulton
Mechanic and inventor	Engineer	Entomologist
Secondary school (Leamington College)	Public school (Sherborne School)	Public school (Marlborough College)
Undistinguished because of dislike of homework	Not known	Not known
R.A.F. apprenticeship, officer training and general flying duties (10 years)	Studies broken by war service (6 years, including 4 years as prisoner of war)	Apprenticeship
Cambridge	Cambridge	Cambridge
R.A.F. apprenticeship as aircraft rigger, flight cadetship and Officers' Engineering Course	Glass process development	Apprenticeship to mechanical engineering
Turbo jet, turbo fan, aft fan, etc. – 35 Turbo drill, etc. – 55	Float glass process – 35	Flexitor torsional shear suspension unit – 28 Rubber cone spring suspension system – 31 Hydrolastic suspension system – 34 Moulton bicycle – 37 Hydrogas suspension system – 52
Military needs. Later industrial challenge	High reward to company for solving technological problems	Desire to create new mechanical things
Chief Engineer	Production Director	Managing Director and Consultant
The Establishment (for jet engine development)	Support, not strife experienced in 'family' business	Support from sponsors but sometimes delay in adoption

TABLE 1 – *continued*

Personal Feature	Wallis	Baker
'Secret' for success	Individual control of relevant technical development work. Personal experience and ability to solve problems. Obsession with problem in hand and persistence	Determination. Application of principles
Attitude to 'group' creativity, i.e. collective problem solving	Nonsense. Creativity is not helped by a group approach	Believes in team work and has experienced creative 'revelation' in a group
Attitude to formal creative thinking techniques	Never tried	Never tried
Attitude to outside financial control	Irksome	—

normal education system and emerge with their creative abilities uninhibited is demonstrated by the paths they followed and their later achievements. Education was essential, nevertheless, for clearly their innovations demanded high technical knowledge and skill which only extensive study and experience could provide. It is significant that the three most 'practical' innovators, Wallis, Whittle and Moulton, all served engineering apprenticeships before pursuing their academic studies and each, in his own way, had earlier experiences which could have strengthened inborn characteristics: Wallis with his free learning experiences at school, Whittle with his opportunities to help his father in making things, and Moulton with his steam car venture.

None of the five produced anything of special note before his late twenties: in each case there seemed to be a long preparation period leading to later achievement. The breadth of achievement and period of time it covered varies quite considerably, but the

Whittle	Pilkington	Moulton
Dedication to solving problems and retaining personal control over technical development	Having the right idea at the right place at the right time	Own master with control over work done. Pragmatic approach to development with maintenance of rapid manufacture and testing of prototypes
All major ideas were personal. Group's duty was to implement them	As a director, sees value in group creativity and encourages it amongst staff	Creative impulse springs from one individual. Transformation of concept into reality requires effective group collaboration
Never tried	Found helpful	Never tried
Adverse effect on development	Shared in control	Excellent working relationship with manufacturing firms sponsoring the development work

secret for success acknowledged by all was personal control over the situation and determination to succeed. Formalized 'creativity', individually or in a group, seemed to have no part in their working style, except for Pilkington, who found it useful and encouraged it in others, though emphasizing the more fundamental need to make people really believe that their creativity was wanted.

The urge to innovate persists in all of them. Barnes Wallis proposes a revolutionary hypersonic aeroplane at eighty-four. John Baker in his seventies helps direct a company to commercialize his ideas. Frank Whittle still has ideas which he believes will have application in the future. Alastair Pilkington, occupied full-time directing a now public firm, still sends ideas to the research laboratory for evaluation. With his latest innovation just launched, Alexander Moulton can contemplate a reduction in his involvement with the creation of new mechanical things some time in the future, but never a complete withdrawal.

All five men have been true innovators. They have not been content to have a brilliant idea and expect other people to take over the drudgery of giving it shape and substance. Each in his own way has exemplified Thomas Edison's statement that genius is one per cent inspiration and ninety-nine per cent perspiration. The inspiration is there to see in their achievements and their stories show that they did not shrink from the other ninety-nine per cent.

All five are aware of their special abilities, though none showed any arrogance over this gift. On the contrary, each discussed his abilities in quite matter-of-fact terms, displaying at the same time a compelling urge to use these gifts. This urge clearly had not enamoured them to their superiors, unless, like Pilkington and Moulton, they were their own bosses. In some ways each appeared to have been able to insulate himself from the outside environment, to be able to follow his own path despite influences around him which would kill any tendency to do likewise in the rest of us.

Though similar in these ways, they appeared to have widely differing styles of working and behaviour. On one hand there was Pilkington, equally successful as an original thinker, a manager of men and director of a large company; the product of the English public school system with hobbies of music, sailing and birds. And Moulton, similar in background, but preferring to work with a small team in a country-house setting to produce the perfect prototype rather than to mass produce, a man perhaps more aware of his thinking process than the rest, pushing logic to its limit and able to go a little bit beyond to produce something recognizably creative. Less concerned with specific practical achievements and more with conceptional innovation was Baker, the backroom boy, working in an academic setting and putting his talents at the disposal of the organization; not really seeking reward, but accepting without diffidence whatever came his way. With his non-industrial background, Whittle was the lone innovator, working on the fringe of a sceptical industry with initially reluctant official support, and struggling with a few influential friends to keep his innovation going under his personal control. And finally Barnes Wallis, who found a secure niche in a large company and so avoided the lonely struggles which faced Whittle; except, of course, when he pursued his self-imposed tasks during the war and now that he is working in retirement.

What seems to emerge from this admittedly inadequate sample of innovators is a rather similar personality pattern of technical adequacy, determination, self-confidence and initiative which is in keeping with part of the profile drawn in Chapter Two. The backgrounds to their innovations and their personal positions relative to them are so different that there are no specific lessons to be learned, except the fundamental one that the true innovator will take the situation as he finds it and achieve his successes either because of it or despite it. Behind each innovator was a team of effective people dedicated to success of his work; willing, it would seem, to be dominated by one man and, figuratively, to become extensions of his limbs in carrying out his wishes.

8 The Effect of Innovation on Society

In previous chapers we have looked at innovation from a number of different standpoints. We shall reverse the process in this final chapter and look outwards at innovation's effects on the environment, in society and the people who form it. Ways of controlling the damage done by some innovation will be considered, and how we can prepare and educate ourselves to encounter the demands made by accelerated growth and change on our powers of assimilation.

As we saw in Chapter Five, technological innovation provokes mixed feelings in most people. In the strictly physical sense man has benefited immensely from it. Clean water, sanitation and improved agricultural methods have raised the living standards of millions and, with a medical service supported by drugs and modern methods of pest control, have increased our life expectancy by thirty years in a century. Creative engineers have given us deaf aids, plastic eye lenses, electronic blood-pressure regulators and artificial heart valves; provided greater mobility, speed and comfort for millions than the richest man on earth enjoyed a hundred years ago; halved the average working week in industrialized countries in 150 years; made it possible to talk and see across the world; helped provide a greater understanding and some small control of the forces of nature such as the weather and earthquakes. Some of the things we accept today without a second thought would appear to be pure magic to our great grandfathers.

On the other hand, still in the strictly physical sense, innovation has put man at peril by upsetting the complex natural balances that maintain the environment in equilibrium. Transport systems, fuel combustion in houses, factories and industrial processes produce fumes which harm man's health, disfigure his buildings and foul his vegetation. From the solid fuel that he burns so wastefully he discharges tons of dust into the atmosphere which, under the right conditions of humidity, form smog and which, some say, may eventually accumulate with natural dust in the atmosphere to form a reflecting barrier to the sun's rays. It may then enter into a dangerous tug of war with another pollutant: the tons of carbon dioxide produced by burning fuels could form an insulating layer in the atmosphere and significantly reduce the natural radiation of heat from the earth's surface. A vital natural balance is thus at risk.

Nature's self-cleansing cycles are overloaded. Rivers are fed with water contaminated with artificial fertilizers, insecticides and detergents; with sewage and industrial effluents; even on occasion with radio-active waste. They are warmed and rewarmed by the use of their water for industrial cooling, progressively reducing the oxygen content and at the same time increasing the rate of oxidation processes, thus cumulatively reducing the amount of oxygen available for decomposing organic matter. Discharging into the sea, the water adds its quota to the build-up of pollution there, affecting the creatures living in it and returning to contaminate man when he eats them.

Man has polluted his environment with noise, making life barely tolerable around airports and busy roads. He has created a monster with his road transport system, which exacts a toll of one person's life every hour and a thousand injured every day in Britain; and imposes a burden of about nine new pence a day on every family in the country for the waste of time and the inefficiency of the system. However horrified he may be at these costs, he cannot easily be rid of them. The car industry is the biggest employer of labour in Britain, earning huge sums of money in exports and providing the mechanical means of moving about 80 per cent of all the manufactured goods in the country. The problems in air transport are just as complex and cannot be solved by any simple means without creating problems elsewhere. London Airport is the third largest port in Britain after London and Liverpool. Twenty million people fly in and out every year and ten million foreign visitors a year are expected in Britain by 1975, spending hundreds of millions of pounds while they are here.

Technological innovation, then, is a mixed blessing. More accurately it is the total system of which innovation is only a part: political decisions determine the direction and pace of change, technological or otherwise, and these decisions ultimately reflect the needs, values and desires of the mass of people subscribing to the policies in force. Innovation need not be damaging in the short or long term unless we allow it to be. It can range from being entirely for our benefit in intention and effect to being the product of a narrowly interested group with little regard to social good, depending on the vigilance, determination and breadth of vision of those entrusted with political power. By legal constraint and financial incentive they can guide and control innovations and areas of change, reflecting in this the moral, aesthetic and humanitarian standards of themselves and those they represent. Such control will not inhibit innovation: on the contrary, by introducing constraints and stringent standards the quality of successful innovation will be raised. Nor need it be without advantage to the innovator in a profit-motivated society just because it is socially beneficial.

It would be wrong to imply that innovation is pursued wilfully to the detriment of the general public, except in the rarest cases. Usually what seems to have been lacking when a brilliant idea becomes a public menace is that all aspects and eventualities have not been foreseen and allowed for before implementation. Ignorance or negligence may be levelled at the innovator, but bad intent scarcely ever. The first jet-propelled passenger transport aeroplane, the De Havilland Comet, met with disaster, but its designers' intentions were surely of the highest. Box girder bridges and DDT were innovations backed by the best of motives, but serious flaws discovered later turned them into calamities.

An innovation which had unexpected and not wholly desirable side effects is described by Rogers and Shoemaker (1971) in a study concerning the introduction of tractors into a number of rural Turkish villages. Hitherto motorized vehicles had been rare, roads poor and communications difficult. The people had led peaceful, slow-moving, traditional lives. With help from the United States, the government introduced thousands of tractors into the area, accompanied by other vehicles and farm implements and supported by a massive road-building programme. A deciding factor in the amount of aid offered was the extent of land owned by each village. Those owning much land bought more tractors than less fortunate ones. Wealthy villagers with large farms likewise outbought their poorer neighbours. Richer communities and individuals had more, got more and produced more still, and the gap between rich and poor was widened. For the whole area better roads and transport brought about widespread changes. Villages became less isolated, towns more accessible for work and recreation. Villagers could work in the towns and commute daily. Migration to the towns began, new houses were built in new styles, habits changed and values with them. Entertainment and food habits altered too. Canned goods and bakery bread replaced home cooking and baking. New shops sprang up and a new economy crept in. Subsistence farming was replaced gradually by growing for commercial markets. There were basic benefits all round, but the new luxuries and comforts which also became available could often be afforded only by the better-off, leaving their poorer neighbours frustrated and hopeless. An innovation intended to bring benefits to a whole community certainly succeeded in its objective, but in doing so disrupted a stable way of life and widened the gap between the haves and the have-nots.

How do we reduce the possibility of ill effects accompanying an innovation? A number of measures seem necessary, designed to see the innovation in its totality by looking backwards, forwards and outwards. In terms of the materials we use we should look at their sources, assess the demands made on irreplaceable elements against the value of the product, and consider the process which must be followed to get the material to the state we need it: and we should look forward to the ultimate disposal of the innovation – can the material be re-used? If not, will it easily return to its natural state? Will it be contaminated, or in any way hazardous? Metals, essential to so many innovations, for instance, are refined, formed into shapes, used during the life of the object and then largely discarded. We throw away over 90 per cent of the aluminium we use, disperse metals such as tungsten and chromium in steel alloys in such small proportions that it is uneconomic to recover them, and discharge a significant proportion of our refined lead into the atmosphere through the combustion of lead-doped petrol. We do recover some of the more expensive metals and others that are easy to reclaim. Some lead is recovered, particularly that from old batteries, and much of our silver is used and re-used. Steel and copper are reclaimed from scrap and re-cycled, but much is lost and the remainder is less than 100 per cent pure. Our fossil fuels have only one life: once burned, coal, gas and oil are lost, their energy dispersing as heat and their constituents largely as pollution into the atmosphere.

We should look at an innovation as a small bit of technological evolution; thinking of its changing impact and value as it develops, and the impression it has on people and groups from different backgrounds. Concorde, through the eyes of the public, its manufacturers, their competitors, government and the treasury, conservationists and anti-pollutionists, engineers and artists, is seen quite differently according to the values of the viewers and the particular moment in time. The noisome back-end view of the aeroplane on take-off evokes a different reaction from its profile in full flight, and its appeal as a prestige achievement contrasts with its appetite for more and more funds to support its development.

Still in terms of evolution, we should question whether a particular innovation establishes a new and artificial equilibrium between man and nature. Much of our technology has this effect: machines provide an essential element in the new balance, and once we become used to the new situation any sudden breakdown could bring about dangerously swift changes. We know the catastrophical effects of the failure of the life-support system in space craft. What of the effects of a failure of the life-support system for one of the predicted two-mile-high skyscraper cities with a population of hundreds of thousands? Clearly we must ensure safety and continuity of use for processes and products if people have become vitally dependent on them. Hazard and operability studies (see page 54) must be obligatory, with an equally searching examination of the total system into which an innovation is to be introduced, to check its source of energy, compatibility with other essential parts, its side effects and so on.

Much can be learned from the meticulous approach of the space industry in America to ensure safety in a complex and wholly interdependent system.

Better still, we can aim to make our innovations harmonize with natural forces and established patterns of living, so that failure does not impose a sudden jerk backwards. At the simple level this could mean having the product, machine, or whatever, made locally instead of making everyone highly dependent upon one efficient but distant point of supply. At a more sophisticated level, it could mean making the innovation as much as possible a development of one of the natural cycles, so that there is a stable system as a back-up should things go wrong. The selective breeding of animals and plants for high food value is one example; the development of bio-degradable plastics in which nature can complete the disposal cycle unaided is another.

Looking at an innovation as an invasion of an existing technological pattern, we should ask what it is intended to replace, partially or wholly; what is needed to support it, and what technically might succeed it; and then we should find ways of making the invasion as painless as possible. Imagine, for instance, a new energy storage system which could be used for powering a motor car – some means of accumulating energy safely and cheaply which can be released under control to drive the car wheels. A conventional electrical storage battery can do this, and so can compressed air: a mechanical flywheel and a spring can do it, and heat can be stored and released in an analogous manner. Let us assume the system uses some thermal storage system, and consider how people in various parts of society will view it. A petrol station owner, whose objective is to make a living out of selling conventional fuels and oil, will see it as a threat to his established mode of business and the whole traditional fuel-vending structure which supports him. With some prompting he may realize that his job really consists in providing energy for motor cars, not just dispensing petrol, and in this new frame of mind he may be able to see opportunities for continuing in business, even profiting from the change. By thinking about the problem from his point of view the innovator could help him to adjust to the new situation, perhaps modifying his product to make it more easily assimilated

TABLE 2: *Reactions to the Introduction of an Imaginary New Energy Source for Motor Vehicles*

Group Affected	Demands by the Group	Possible Responses by the Innovator	Actions by the Innovator to Ease Acceptance
Drivers	Make driving cheaper and safer	It will be cheaper, and pilfer-proof, non-toxic and fume-free	
	Make it possible to install the new energy system into existing vehicles	It will be too expensive to do this, but new cars incorporating the new system will be cheaper	Minimize the changes needed and provide clear instructions for them
	Don't make me have to learn new driving skills	Driving will be almost unchanged. Refuelling will be as simple as refilling with petrol	
Community	Reduce fumes, smell, noise	The only exhaust will be steam and adequate silencing will be provided	Use this fact in publicity
	Reduce the cost of roads	This system will not affect the cost of roads: indeed its advantages will probably lead to an increase in road transport	
Government	Keep within the law	We will check all statutory requirements applying to the new system	Use this fact in publicity
	Conserve natural resources	The basic source of energy will be natural gas instead of oil	
	National income must be maintained, and the new system will have to be taxed to make up for	We feel powerless to affect this but suggest the new system should be allowed to remain	Provide government and public bodies with facts

		gradual. There is an increasing demand for oil for other uses. Why not join in the exploitation of the innovation?	offer co-operation in development of the system
Petrol stations	Let us serve the new system with minimum change to our way of working and to our installations	There will be a need for replenishment stations and we will work with you to develop a mutually satisfactory system	Provide full information and offer co-operation in development of the system
Vehicle manufacturers	Make manufacture easier and cheaper. Bring us into the development as soon as possible	We will work with you to develop an integrated system	Provide full information and offer co-operation in development of the system
Repair mechanics	Teach us about the new system and help us to develop the skills needed	We will do this through the car manufacturers	Provide full information and offer co-operation in development of the system
Component suppliers	Tell us exactly what you want. Bring us in as early as possible and let us share in the development	We will explain what it is we are trying to do and will use your knowledge and skill as much as possible	Provide full information and offer co-operation in development of the system
Other innovators	We will invent around your idea and reduce your lead time as much as we can.	We expect invasion and will protect ourselves by patents, at the same time trying to keep ahead with new ideas and improvements	Provide full information and offer co-operation in development of the system
	We have ideas which could be complementary to yours.	Let us keep in touch and help each other to mutual success	Provide full information and offer co-operation in development of the system

into the standard petrol station layout. There are many other groups that would be affected by this same innovation. Sometimes there would be cross-linkages, too, for example between car manufacturers, the driving public and repair mechanics. But let us just look at the innovators and direct interaction with them. Table 2 shows some of the main points of contact.

Clearly such an innovation in energy would not be assimilated without effort and problems. But by approaching it as a change in the *total* system and involving as many interested parties as possible, helping them to see problems as opportunities for gain on both sides rather than a struggle for advantage, there would be much greater prospects of success.

Innovation means change, and change absorbs a lot of physical, mental and emotional energy. Decimal coinage was a comparatively simple innovation, but it took a lot of effort on everybody's part before it was established and people began to feel comfortable with the new system. North Sea gas is still a nuisance to many people. There has to be some human adjustment whenever something new is introduced and there will be people who will have to pay a lot in human terms for comparatively little in return.

In the early 1800s the Luddites raised riots in this country to destroy machinery which threatened their livelihood. Only recently the dockers reacted against the containerization of goods for the same reason. In the example of the hypothetical energy source discussed above, several important questions bearing on individual and group wellbeing remained unanswered, and if we look at other areas in which technological growth is rapid it is clear that the changes will inevitably be accompanied by problems and doubts enough to raise the resistance of many reasonable people. The problem of the motor car has been discussed already. We have computers capable of storing enormous amounts of information, with potential for misuse by unscrupulous people. Medicine and technology have worked wonders to keep people alive, so increasing their chance of dying of starvation. Chemical engineering has given us new and useful materials, which will not disappear when we have finished with them. Automation and mechanization have made hard labour a thing of the past for millions of people, but have left some without a job at all.

Despite these penalties, however, innovation is going on continually, and gives the impression of having a momentum of its own. Man must innovate, for he has already evolved a technology which allows him some independence of his environment, but an independence which is under constant challenge and needs continuing readjustment to maintain it. And he must innovate because society will demand it of him. Toynbee (1966) reminds us that when Gandhi advocated the rejection of Western technology in India and a return to a non-technological culture his advice was ignored, despite the reverence in which he was held. Imagine the reaction to any suggestion that the nations of the world should stop all innovation right now . . . Yes, but first we must conquer the food shortage, cure cancer, improve our whole transport system, stop polluting our rivers . . .

Each innovation can become a source in itself for further development, a springboard for other leaps forward in one or more directions, giving a rate of development akin to an exponential growth whose rate at any time depends on its size at that time. Looking forward, the rate of development is always greater than looking backward. Well before the time of Christ, lodestone was known for its magnetic properties, but not until A.D. 1100 were artificial magnets made by stroking pieces of iron with lodestone. Then in the nineteenth century a few vital discoveries and inventions occurred, including the electrolytic cell for producing direct current, and the principle of magnetic induction. From these seed points developed, slowly at first, the electric motor, transformer, electro-magnet, telegraph, telephone and electric bell: then with increasing tempo as linkages with other technical achievements were made, the radio, magnetic tape recorder, television, computer, radar, navigation aids – in fact, the whole electronics explosion.

This mushrooming of growth, as the periphery of achievement increases at an accelerating rate owing to its own seeding process of knowledge and opportunity, is found in other technologies. It is shown graphically for the field of flight in Fig. 14. The astonishing acceleration of progress in the last 100 years compared with the rest of recorded history is plain to see, and there is no reason to believe that any of the branches shown has reached its

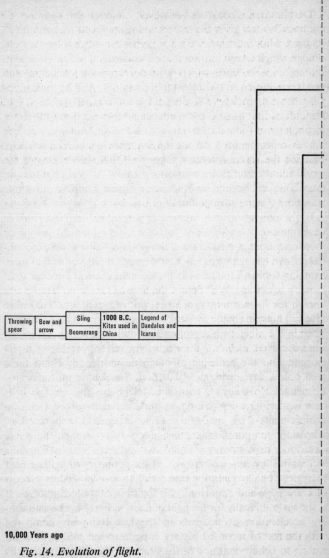

| Throwing spear | Bow and arrow | Sling | 1000 B.C. Kites used in China | Legend of Daedalus and Icarus |
| Boomerang |

10,000 Years ago

Fig. 14. Evolution of flight.

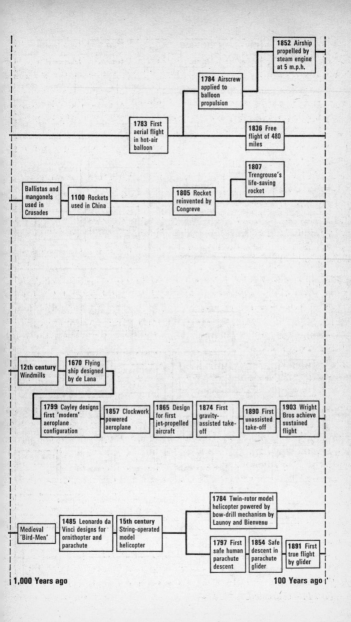

1852 Airship propelled by steam engine at 5 m.p.h.

1784 Airscrew applied to balloon propulsion

1783 First aerial flight in hot-air balloon

1836 Free flight of 480 miles

1807 Trengrouse's life-saving rocket

Ballistas and mangonels used in Crusades

1100 Rockets used in China

1805 Rocket reinvented by Congreve

12th century Windmills

1670 Flying ship designed by de Lana

1799 Cayley designs first 'modern' aeroplane configuration

1857 Clockwork powered aeroplane

1865 Design for first jet-propelled aircraft

1874 First gravity-assisted take-off

1890 First unassisted take-off

1903 Wright Bros achieve sustained flight

Medieval 'Bird-Men'

1485 Leonardo da Vinci designs for ornithopter and parachute

15th century String-operated model helicopter

1784 Twin-rotor model helicopter powered by bow-drill mechanism by Launoy and Bienvenu

1797 First safe human parachute descent

1854 Safe descent in parachute glider

1891 First true flight by glider

1,000 Years ago

100 Years ago

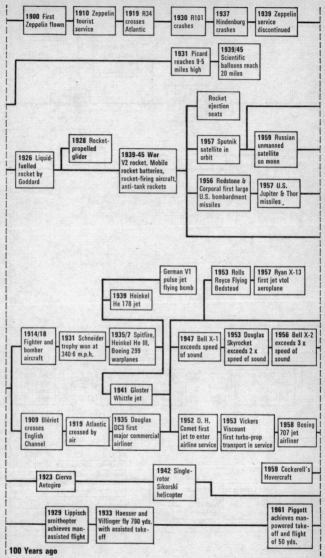

1900 First Zeppelin flown | **1910** Zeppelin tourist service | **1919** R34 crosses Atlantic | **1930** R101 crashes | **1937** Hindenburg crashes | **1939** Zeppelin service discontinued

1931 Picard reaches 9·5 miles high | **1939/45** Scientific balloons reach 20 miles

Rocket ejection seats

1926 Liquid-fuelled rocket by Goddard | **1928** Rocket-propelled glider | **1939–45 War** V2 rocket. Mobile rocket batteries, rocket-firing aircraft, anti-tank rockets | **1957** Sputnik satellite in orbit | **1959** Russian unmanned satellite on moon

1956 Redstone & Corporal first large U.S. bombardment missiles | **1957** U.S. Jupiter & Thor missiles

German V1 pulse jet flying bomb | **1953** Rolls Royce Flying Bedstead | **1957** Ryan X-13 first jet vtol aeroplane

1939 Heinkel He 178 jet

1914/18 Fighter and bomber aircraft | **1931** Schneider trophy won at 340·6 m.p.h. | **1935/7** Spitfire, Heinkel He III, Boeing 299 warplanes | **1947** Bell X-1 exceeds speed of sound | **1953** Douglas Skyrocket exceeds 2 x speed of sound | **1956** Bell X-2 exceeds 3 x speed of sound

1941 Gloster Whittle jet

1909 Blériot crosses English Channel | **1919** Atlantic crossed by air | **1935** Douglas DC3 first major commercial airliner | **1952** D. H. Comet first jet to enter airline service | **1953** Vickers Viscount first turbo-prop transport in service | **1958** Boeing 707 jet airliner

1923 Cierva Autogiro | **1942** Single-rotor Sikorski helicopter | **1959** Cockerell's Hovercraft

1929 Lippisch ornithopter achieves man-assisted flight | **1933** Haesser and Villinger fly 790 yds. with assisted take-off | **1961** Piggott achieves man-powered take-off and flight of 50 yds.

100 Years ago

Fig. 14 – continued.

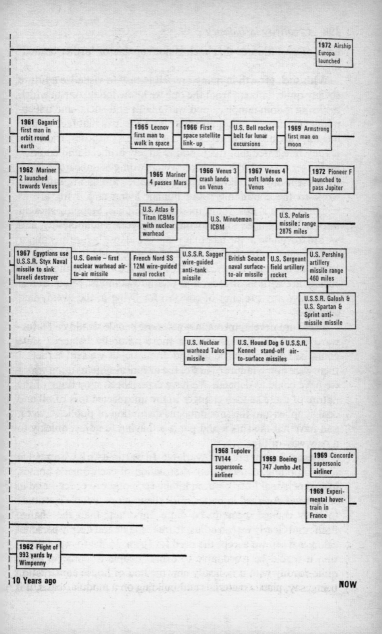

1972 Airship Europa launched

1961 Gagarin first man in orbit round earth

1965 Leonov first man to walk in space

1966 First space satellite link- up

U.S. Bell rocket belt for lunar excursions

1969 Armstrong first man on moon

1962 Mariner 2 launched towards Venus

1965 Mariner 4 passes Mars

1966 Venus 3 crash lands on Venus

1967 Venus 4 soft lands on Venus

1972 Pioneer F launched to pass Jupiter

U.S. Atlas & Titan ICBMs with nuclear warhead

U.S. Minuteman ICBM

U.S. Polaris missile: range 2875 miles

1967 Egyptians use U.S.S.R. Styx Naval missile to sink Israeli destroyer

U.S. Genie – first nuclear warhead air-to-air missile

French Nord SS 12M wire-guided naval rocket

U.S.S.R. Sagger wire-guided anti-tank missile

British Seacat naval surface-to-air missile

U.S. Sergeant field artillery rocket

U.S. Pershing artillery missile range 460 miles

U.S.S.R. Galosh & U.S. Spartan & Sprint anti-missile missile

U.S. Nuclear warhead Talos missile

U.S. Hound Dog & U.S.S.R. Kennel stand-off air-to-surface missiles

1968 Tupolev TV144 supersonic airliner

1969 Boeing 747 Jumbo Jet

1969 Concorde supersonic airliner

1969 Experimental hover-train in France

1962 Flight of 993 yards by Wimpenny

10 Years ago

NOW

limit of evolution or that each is not capable of further branching.

With such growth in many areas it is easy to visualize a future society quite different from the one we know today, one in which recycling is commonplace and waste both anti-social and uneconomic; electronic communication is so effective that face-to-face meetings are no longer necessary for business purposes; transport is fully integrated and free; food is largely artificial and cooking no longer an art but a science; overcrowding is unbearably high by present-day standards; leisure activities are as important as work to the community; and human living and dying are as regulated as it is now for domesticated animals. Stepping straight into such a changed society would tax anyone's adaptability, and we are fortunate in the fact that years will elapse before any major evolutionary technological or social change could become established throughout the system. However, the seeds of this future society are with us already, and their growth must be controlled if we have any pretence of concern for living in the twenty-first century.

These are developments in what most people would call a forward direction. Reversion to a more naturally balanced state could be much more sudden and dramatic, as we said earlier, there were ever a failure of one of the technical systems upon which we have come to depend. We have experienced something of the nature of these sudden changes in the unexpected loss of oil and coal supplies and the simultaneous disruption of public services; and have felt the shock and panic at having to adjust quickly to a new way of life.

These reactions are not invariable. In wartime we have accepted food rationing, conscription, destruction of each other's homes, loss of personal liberty – even killing each other to order – and in some ways emerged in better spirit than before. People's attitude towards change seems to be more important than the change itself; and clearly we can adjust to quite major and deeply personal changes when we accept the need for them. In the forward direction it would be reasonable to expect people to come to terms quite readily with a radically new method of house construction using, say, plastic materials and building on a modular basis, if it eliminated our chronic housing shortage, even though it might also revolutionize the building industry and force residents to adjust to novel structures and materials. Accommodation to the physical changes would be achieved easily because they would be satisfying a felt human need. On the other hand, the imposition of all the possibilities of technology to the regulation and maintenance of human life, to the extent of determining how and when we should live and die, would be resisted because this would be too great an infringement on our personal values. Today, for instance, the introduction of birth control as a means of reducing population growth is resisted strongly by those whose religion condemns it or whose male virility is proved by the procreation of children.

More immediately important for living today is the cumulative effect of a multitude of small bits of change which are being imposed upon us by the accelerating growth of new technology, each technical development making its demand for small adjustments in our working habits, skill, style of living or expectations. The profusion of new processes and products has already increased radically the amount of novelty in our lives, shortened the duration of stable systems and packed more and more changing experience into every day, week and month. This increasingly transient nature of society is exemplified in throw-away containers and clothing, built-in obsolescence in motor cars and appliances, portable architecture (our art, too, is acquiring mobility and aspects of impermanence), rented clothing, new brands of food and playthings (remember the hula-hoop, the super-ball and clackers?). Even the news is out of date within hours. If changes occur too fast and too frequently people's ability to adjust will be overstretched and they will lose contact with part or the whole of the reality of the situation. Personal landmarks will be lost, says Schon (1970), and perceptions of the wider environment will become more fragmented and less likely to be shared by others, adds Vickers (1968). In this state of increased isolation and uncertainty, the person's sense of identity will be weakened and with it his feelings of security and direction. He may try to re-establish the old structure by clinging to old ways and decrying the new. Or he may just opt out, the victim in the ultimate of what Toffler (1970) calls 'future shock', the 'shattering stress and disorientation that we induce in individuals by subjecting them to too much change in too short a time'.

Unfortunately, the innovator contributes unnecessarily to the changes imposed on people by his tendency to stress the novel aspects of his work. However, if he heeds Toffler, he will reduce the mystery and newness surrounding the change by describing and introducing it in such a way that its unfamiliar features are *minimized* and it is seen as just a step in the natural progression of accepted patterns of work and living. Most innovations contain more that is well tried and familiar than is truly novel. Sometimes little more than the presentation and jargon is new. It might be unprofitable to the innovator to paint a true picture, but it could be healthier for society to play the novelty down. And however small the change, time must be allowed for it to be assimilated, even when the change is clearly beneficial and contains no personal threat or social upheaval. Habits and attitudes, good or bad, need time to undo as well as to develop. Failure to bring about rapid change may not be due to resistance or inertia, but just a very time-consuming need to re-adjust. Temperature in degrees Centigrade is still an alien measure to most adult people in Britain, despite its simple and logical scale.

So far we have concerned ourselves with the effects of innovation on people in society in general, and what can be done to reduce the harmful ecological and human side effects accompanying it. Industry, the user as well as the originator of so much innovation, has special problems in maintaining a healthy human climate in the face of the frequent changes it imposes upon itself. To be able to mobilize sufficient energy to adjust quickly and flexibly to these changes, members of a working group must be well integrated and working to a common purpose which is clearly understood and accepted by all; be able to analyse realistically the situation in which they find themselves; be committed to the specific actions decided upon; and learn from experience. The characteristics of the innovative group that we discussed in Chaper Six are also those required in any group faced with adaptation to change.

One of the problems of imposed change on a group is the different rates at which individual members can adjust to it. We may find managers well able to keep abreast of the changes going on around them because of their training, experience and opportunities for seeing the broad picture; while their less favourably placed subordinates are tied much closer to the processes and standards they grew up with. The resulting gap can only be bridged by managers taking the initiative to give information and offer opportunities for learning the new realities, backed by support and understanding during the period of readjustment.

Sometimes an innovation will create a mismatch between the job pattern and the social system uniting the people who have to work to it. Trist and his co-authors (1963) describe the effect of installing the longwall method of cutting coal in British mines in place of the old shortwall system. In the latter a small group of up to eight men worked as a team in one section of the coal face, the team having complete autonomy for cutting, loading and removing the coal under a leader of its own choosing. Membership of the team was by mutual selection and relationships were close, including an acceptance of team responsibility towards a member's family if he was killed or injured. With the introduction of the longwall method, larger teams of forty to fifty men were required on a shift basis and the men were spread out over the full width of the seam. New differentials were introduced and the method of working changed to mechanized mass production. Disruption of the old group relationships, changes in prestige and reduction in effective supervision resulted in a loss of meaning in the job and a feeling of indifference, accompanied by a new norm of low productivity. These difficulties were only removed by giving satisfying social and emotional relationships back to the miners by redesigning the formal organization and method of working.

In America more recently, groups of people from varying backgrounds have formed self-contained communities with a prime aim of integrating work and living, and have found that this not only brings people closer together but actually releases extra energy and skills. In such communities, Mosher (1973) comments, alienation from work is avoided by taking control of the situation and shaping the physical and social environment to satisfy the needs of individuals and the group.

Technological innovation such as automation, computer control and assembly-line processes sometimes removes the need for human skill and effort: a desirable aim in many ways, but one which deprives people of work that is stimulating and satisfying. They leave the operator with a dull and boring job with control of pace and sequence taken from him and vested in the machine. Although the effects of this can be lessened by including other duties, such as inspection and testing, by providing opportunities for making creative contributions to the whole job and by job rotation, such innovation inevitably cuts the total amount of satisfying work available.

The problem, therefore, includes getting the rate of change and the stimulation it provides at a healthy and satisfying level: too high and workers begin to lose touch; too low and they become bored and sluggish, waiting only for release from a mental slow motion, or introducing some excitement just to break the tedium – horseplay, fighting the system, etc. Good process and work design should reduce the need for people to do tedious work, and growing opportunities for exercising talents outside must offer compensation for those who remain.

In a general environment which threatens to be too full of complexity and change, however, preserving individual wellbeing will call for a deeper personal effort. We can learn from the behaviour of those who already cope with the stress of change. Travellers who fly across the Atlantic allow their biological time to adjust to the sudden leap forward or backward in local time before taking important decisions. Those who must move constantly from one place to another preserve some thread of stability in their lives by forming personal habits which they keep to wherever they are, and staying in the same place whenever they return. Some of them set aside half an hour each day for quiet meditation as a means of maintaining personal tranquillity and developing an awareness of the things that are universal and unchanging. By building a safe and stable personal framework, with security drawn from inner resources rather than other people, they are able to live with flux around them. Whatever their particular solution, all seem to be striving for security of their personal identity, as a means of coping with the turmoil of living today.

To see normal human beings coping with quite enormous amounts of novelty, we need only look at the process of learning and development in children. In twenty odd years they develop from a state of helpless ignorance to one in which they can use the recorded knowledge of their whole evolution, aided by curiosity, a unique manipulative dexterity and a tremendous capacity to learn. They fill in the 'blank tablet' of their infant mind with personal experience by observing, experimenting and innovating – innovating in the internal and personal sense of translating newly discovered concepts into useful bits of mental and physical skill. During their early years, change is the natural order. Everything is new and a few more novelties coming along are easily assimilated with the rest. Superconductivity, C.S. gas, probes on Mars and heart transplants are all facts of life to a ten-year-old. They are not an intrusion into his personal living, but part of it immediately he becomes aware of them.

The pliability of childhood in less hectic times is the vehicle by which man has been able to absorb change without stress although, as Piaget (page 46) has shown, there is a natural tendency for this pliability to diminish as the child approaches maturity. At a time when he is overburdened with continuing change, this capacity for imaginative adjustment must be preserved as far as possible throughout adult life. Harrison's work on the development of creativity in children described in Chapter Five gives a hint of what can be achieved, and the methods for personality development in Chapter Four are all designed to free the individual from the mental and emotional blocks to creative and adaptive behaviour that have been learned in the growing-up process.

In Chapter One we suggested that one way of looking at creativity was as the achievement of a more satisfying and complete integration of all the elements in a problem. The same process of establishing a new harmony and stability out of disorder and change is called for in an environment which is in a state of continuing turmoil. Thus, learning to be creative is also learning to be adaptive, and our educational system must provide suitable conditions in which this can happen. Learning to learn should be paramount, so that it becomes a life-long, self-motivated skill enabling the individual to keep himself up to date and to take stock realistically of the changing situation. What is offered for learning should include a value system which places a premium for each updating and renewal. Personal experience should be given in getting to the heart of problems while also taking the broad view when seeking solutions, so that the technical, social and economic aspects all receive due emphasis. Education should be for the whole individual, with personality development as important as the acquisition of knowledge and skill. Maslow's 'self-actualizing person' could be our model.

We should be interested in the question 'What have you learned?', but just as interested in 'What have you learned about yourself?'

We are approaching the situation in which we can achieve physically almost anything we want to through technology, but the price we may have to pay in human stress caused by the accompanying change is high. Our wellbeing depends on our ability to maintain a healthy balance between technological advance and the development of effective personal and organizational strategies to deal with it. Fresh thinking is needed and new concepts in adaptation, which will result in social innovations touching the life of everyone. A good start might be to shift the emphasis from the narrow vision of the affluent society towards the healthier and safer acceptance of the innovative society.

References

Abercrombie, M. L. J., 'Innovation and Training', presented at the Council of Industrial Design Conference 'Innovation in Design', London, 11 February 1971.

Allport, G. W., *Pattern and Growth in Personality*, Holt, New York, 1961.

'American Society for Engineering Education', Final Report of the Goals Committee, January 1968, p. 16.

Amman, R., 'Science in Russian Industry', *New Scientist*, 20 February 1969, pp. 409–10.

Bono, E. de, *The Use of Lateral Thinking*, Jonathan Cape, 1967; Penguin Books, 1971.
  The Mechanism of Mind, Jonathan Cape, 1969; Penguin Books, 1971.
  Lateral Thinking for Management, McGraw-Hill, 1971.

Bouladon, G., 'The Transport Gaps', *Science Journal*, April 1967.

Bright, J. R., 'Evaluating Signals of Technological Change', *Harvard Business Review*, January–February 1970, pp. 62–70.

Bruner, J. S., 'The Conditions of Creativity', in Gruber, H. E., Terrell, G., and Wertheimer, M. (eds.), *Contemporary Approaches to Creative Thinking*, Atherton Press, New York, 1962.

Burnet, Sir Macfarlane, 'After the Age of Discovery', *New Scientist*, 9 December 1971, pp. 96–100.

Burns, T., and Stalker, G. M., *The Management of Innovation*, Tavistock, 1961.

Cairncross, Sir Alec, Presidential Address to the British Association, 1971.

Carr, R. T., 'Applying Knowledge to Practical Purposes', *Chartered Mechanical Engineer*, Vol. 13, No. 6, 1966, pp. 274–9.

Cattell, R. B., 'Theory of Fluid and Crystallized Intelligence: A Critical Experiment', *Journal of Educational Psychology*, Vol. 54, 1963, pp. 1–22.

Chambers, J. C., Mullick, S. K., and Smith, D. D., 'How to Choose the Right Forecasting Technique', *Harvard Business Review*, July–August 1971, pp. 45–74.

Coleman, J. P., 'Helping Inventive Engineers', *Institution of Electrical Engineers, Electronics and Power*, 6 September 1973, p. 362.

Crompton, S., Extract of letter written by Samuel Crompton to John Kennedy dated 30 December 1802, quoted in *Engineering Heritage*, Vol. 1, Institution of Mechanical Engineers, 1963.

Doppelt, J. E., 'Definitions of Creativity', *Transactions of New York Academy of Science*, Series II, Vol. 26, 1964, pp. 788–93.

Eyring, H., 'Scientific Creativity', in Anderson H. H. (ed.), *Creativity and its Cultivation*, Harper and Row, New York, 1959.

Fange, E. K. von, *Professional Creativity*, Prentice-Hall, Englewood Cliffs, New Jersey, 1959.

Flavell, J. H., *The Developmental Psychology of Jean Piaget*, Van Nostrand, Princeton, 1963.

Freeman, C., 'Industrial Innovation: The Key to Success', *Institution of Electrical Engineers, Electronics and Power*, August 1971, pp. 297–301.
  Success and Failure in Industrial Innovation, Centre for the Study of Industrial Innovation, University of Sussex, 1972.

Freud, S., 'A General Introduction to Psychoanalysis', 1920, in Vernon, P. E. (ed.), *Creativity*, Penguin Books, 1970.

Getzels, J. W., and Jackson, P. W., *Creativity and Intelligence: Explorations with Gifted Students*, Wiley, New York, 1962.

Golovin, N. E., 'The Creative Person in Science', in Taylor, C. W., and Barron, F. (eds.), *Scientific Creativity*, Wiley, New York, 1963.

Gordon, T. J., and Helmer, O., *Report on a Long Range Forecasting Study*, Rand Corporation, Santa Monica, California, 1964.

Gordon, W. J. J., *Synectics*, Harper and Row, New York, 1961.

Guilford, J. P., 'Some Recent Findings on Thinking Abilities and their Implications', *Information Bulletin*, Vol. 3, 1952, pp. 48–61.
  'Traits in Creativity', in Anderson H. H. (ed.), *Creativity and its Cultivation*, Wiley, New York, 1959.
  'Intellectual Resources and their Values as Seen by Scientists', in Taylor, C. W., and Barron, F. (eds.), *Scientific Creativity*, Wiley, New York, 1963.

'Basic Problems in Teaching for Creativity', presented at the Conference on Creativity and Teaching Media at La Jolla, California, 31 August–3 September 1964, in McPherson, J. H., *The People, the Problems and the Problem Solving Methods*, Pendell, Midland, Michigan, 1967.

Harding, R. E. M., *An Anatomy of Inspiration*, Frank Cass, 1967.

Harrison, A., 'Developing Autonomy Initiative and Risk-Taking through a Laboratory Design', *European Training*, Vol. 2, No. 2, 1973, pp. 100–16.

Harrison, G. B., 'Technological Creativity at School', in Gregory, S. A. (ed.), *Creativity and Innovation in Engineering*, Butterworths, 1972.

Hebb, D. O., *The Organisation of Behaviour*, Wiley, New York, 1949.

Henle, M., 'The Birth and Death of Ideas', in Gruber, H. E., Terrell, G., and Wertheimer, M. (eds.), *Contemporary Approaches to Creative Thinking*, Atherton Press, New York, 1962.

Herzberg, F., Mausner, B., and Snyderman, B., *The Motivation to Work*, Wiley, New York, 1959.

Hitt, W. D., 'Towards a Two-Factor Theory of Creativity', *Psychological Record*, Vol. 15, 1965, pp. 127–32.

Hudson, L., *Contrary Imaginations*, Methuen, 1966.

Hutchinson, E. D., *How to Think Creatively*, Abingdon Cokesburg, New York, 1949.

Jenkins, G. M., 'The Systems Approach', *Journal of Systems Engineering*, Vol. 1, No. 1, Autumn 1969.

Jones, J. C., *Design Methods – Seeds of Human Futures*, Wiley, New York, 1970.

Kahn, H., and Wiener, A. J., *The Year 2000*, Macmillan, New York, 1967.

Katz, I., 'Recommendations for Eliciting New Ideas from Creative People and Encouraging their Innovation to a Point of Contractual Support', Second Conference on Planetology and Space Mission Planning, New York Academy of Science, December 1967.

Kepner, C. H., and Tregoe, B. B., *The Rational Manager*, McGraw-Hill, New York, 1965.

Knapp, R. H., 'Demographic Cultural and Personality Attributes of Scientists', in Taylor, C. W., and Barron, F. (eds.), *Scientific Creativity*, Wiley, New York, 1963.

Koestler, A., *The Act of Creation*, Hutchinson, 1964.

Kubie, L. S., *Neurotic Distortion of the Creative Process*, University of Kansas Press, Lawrence, 1958.

Kuhn, T. S., 'The Essential Tension: Tradition and Innovation in Scientific Research', in Taylor, C. W., and Barron, F. (eds.), *Scientific Creativity: Its Recognition and Development*, Wiley, New York, 1963.

Land, E., 'Experiments in Color Vision', *Scientific American*, May 1969, pp. 84–99.

Lasswell, H. D., 'The Social Setting of Creativity', in Anderson, H. H. (ed.), *Creativity and its Cultivation*, Harper and Row, New York, 1959.

Lewin, K., *A Dynamic Theory of Personality*, McGraw-Hill, New York, 1935.

Field Theory in Social Sciences; Selected Theoretical Papers, ed. D. Cartright, Harper, New York, 1951.

Likert, R., *New Patterns in Management*, McGraw-Hill, New York, 1961.

Lloyd, N. E., Private correspondence quoted in McPherson, J. H., *The People, The Problems and the Problem Solving Methods*, Pendell, Midland, Michigan, 1967, pp. 38–40.

Low, I., 'The Facts of Technological Life', *New Scientist*, 9 May 1968, p. 296.

McClelland, D. C., *The Achieving Society*, Van Nostrand, Princeton, 1961.

'Towards a Theory of Motive Acquisition', *American Psychologist*, XX, No. 2, 1965, pp. 321–33.

McGregor, D. M., *The Human Side of Enterprise*, McGraw-Hill, New York, 1960.

MacKinnon, D. W., 'Fostering Creativity in Students of Engineering', *Journal of Engineering Education*, Vol. 52, 1961, pp. 129–42.

Mackler, B., and Shontz, F. C., 'Creativity: Theoretical and Methodological Considerations', *Psychological Record*, Vol. 15, 1965, pp. 217–38.

Mackworth, N. H., 'Originality', *American Psychologist*, Vol. 20, No. 1, pp. 51–66, 1965.

McPherson, J. H., 'How to Manage Creative Engineers', *Mechanical Engineering*, February 1965, pp. 32–6.

The People, the Problems and the Problem Solving Methods, Pendell, Midland, Michigan, 1967.

Maddi, S. R., 'Motivational Aspects of Creativity', *Journal of Personality*, Vol. 33, 1965, pp. 330–47.

Maier, N. R. F., 'An Aspect of Human Reasoning', *British Journal of Psychology*, Vol. 24, 1933, pp. 144–55.

Maslow, A., *Motivation and Personality*, Harper and Row, New York, 1954.

'Creativity in Self-Actualising People', in Anderson H. H. (ed.), *Creativity and its Cultivation*, Harper and Row, New York, 1959.

Matchett, E., 'Control of Thought in Creative Work', *Chartered Mechanical Engineer*, Vol. 15, No. 4, 1968, pp. 163–6.

'Extending the Designer's Mental Powers', *Institution of Electrical Engineers, Electronics and Power*, February 1971, pp. 67–72.

Mencher, A. G., 'Two Strategies for Research and Development Managers', *Science Journal*, June 1969, pp. 81–3.

Mogenson, A. H., 'Mogy's Work Simplification is Working New Miracles', *Factory*, September 1965.

Moore, A. D., *Invention, Discovery and Creativity*, Doubleday, New York, 1969.

Moore, P. G., 'A Survey of Operational Research', *Journal of the Royal Statistical Society*, A129, 399, 1966.

Morison, E., *Men, Machines and Modern Times*, M.I.T. Press, Boston, 1966.

Mosher, C. R., 'One: An Urban Community', *Journal of Applied Behavioral Science*, Vol. 9, No. 2/3, March/June 1973, pp. 218, 232.

Moulton, A. E., 'Craftsmanship and Life', First Lucas Annual Lecture, Joseph Lucas Ltd., Birmingham, 1965.

'Creativity in Engineering', talk given at Institution of Mechanical Engineers, London, 31 October 1968.

Murray, H. A., *Thematic Apperception Test Manual*, Harvard University Press, 1943.

Nadler, G., *Works Systems Design: The Ideals Concept*, Richard D. Irwin, Homewood, Illinois, 1967.

North, H. Q., and Pyke, D. L., 'Probes of the Technological Future', *Harvard Business Review*, May–June 1969, pp. 68–82.

Osborn, A. F., *Applied Imagination*, Charles Scribner, 1953.

Osgood, C. E., *Method and Theory in Experimental Psychology*, Oxford University Press, 1953.

Parnes, S. J., 'Education and Creativity', *Teachers College Record*, Vol. 64, 1963, pp. 331–9.

Parnes, S. J., and Brunelle, E. A., 'The Literature of Creativity (Part I)', *Journal of Creative Behavior*, Vol. 1, 1967, pp. 52–7.

Paul, W. J., Robertson, K. B., and Herzberg, F., 'Job Enrichment Pays Off', *Harvard Business Review*, March–April 1969, pp. 61–78.

Pelz, D. C., 'Creative Tensions in the Research and Development Climate', *Science* Vol. 157, No. 3785, 14 July 1967, pp. 160–65.

Pelz, D. C., and Andrews, F. M., *Scientists in Organisations – Productive Climates for Research and Development*, Wiley, New York, 1966.

Pfeiffer, J. W., and Jones, J. E., *A Handbook of Structural Experiences for Human Relations Training*, Vol. III, University Associates Press, Iowa, 1971.

Pilkington, L. A. B., 'The Float Glass Process', Review Lecture, *Proceedings of the Royal Society*, Vol. 314A, 1969, pp. 1–25.

Prince, G. M., 'The Operational Mechanisms of Synectics', *Journal of Creative Behaviour*, Vol. 2, No. 1, 1968.

  'How to Be a Better Meeting Chairman', *Harvard Business Review*, January–February 1969, pp. 98–108.

Raudsepp, E., 'Forcing Ideas with Synectics – A Creative Approach to Problem Solving', *Machine Design*, 16 October 1969, pp. 134–9.

Reynolds, Sir Joshua, quoted in Offner, D. H., 'Energising the Creative Potential in Future Engineers', *Journal of Creative Behaviour*, Vol. 1, 1967, pp. 15–21.

Rickers-Ovsiankena, M. A., 'Studies in the Personality Structures of Schizophrenic Individuals: II Reactions to Interrupted Tasks, *Journal of Genetic Psychology*, Vol. 16, 1937, pp. 179–96.

Roberts, E. B., and Wainer, H. A., 'New Enterprises on Route 128', *Science Journal*, December 1968, pp. 78–83.

Rogers, C. R., 'Towards a Theory of Personality', in Anderson H. H. (ed.), *Creativity and its Cultivation*, Harper and Row, New York, 1959.

  'The Characteristics of a Helping Relationship', in Bennis, W. G., Benne, K. D., and Chin, R. (eds.), *The Planning of Change*, Holt, Rinehart and Winston, 1961.

Rogers, E. M., and Shoemaker, F. F., *Communication of Innovations*, Cross Cultural Approach, Free Press, 1971.

Schon, D., *Beyond the Stable State*, Temple South, 1970.

Shapiro, E. J., 'The Identification of Creative Research Scientists', *Psychologia Africana*, II, 1966, pp. 99–132.

Simone, D. V. de, 'Education for Innovation', *I.E.E.E. Spectrum*, Vol. 5, No. 1, January 1968, pp. 83–9.

Sinnott, E. W., 'The Creativeness of Life', in Anderson H. H. (ed.), *Creativity and its Cultivation*, Harper and Row, New York, 1959.

Smith, E. P., 'The Manager as an Action Central Leader', *The Industrial Society*, 1969.

Spearman, C., *Abilities of Man*, Macmillan, New York, 1927.

Stedman, J., 'Engineering and the Many Cultures', in Simone, D. V. de (ed.), *Education for Innovation*, Pergamon, 1968.

Stein, M. I., 'A Transactional Approach to Creativity', in Taylor, C. W., and Barron, E. (eds.), *Scientific Creativity*, Wiley, New York, 1963.

Tannenbaum, R., and Schmidt, W. H., 'How to Choose a Leadership Pattern', *Harvard Business Review*, March–April, 1958, pp. 95–101.

Thurstone, L. L., and Thurstone, T. G., *Factorial Studies of Intelligence*, University of Chicago Press, Chicago, 1941.

Toffler, A., *Future Shock*, Random House, New York, 1970.

Toynbee, A. J., *Change and Habit*, Oxford University Press, 1966.

Trist, E., Higgin, G., Murray, H., and Pollack, A., *Organisational Choice*, Tavistock, 1963.

United States Department of Commerce, *Technological Innovation: Its Environment and Management*, U.S. Government Printing Office, Washington, 1967.

Vernon, P. E. (ed.), *Creativity*, Penguin Books, 1970.

Vickers, G., *Value Systems and Social Process*, Tavistock, 1968.

Wallack, M. A., and Kogan, N., *Modes of Thinking in Young Children*, Holt, Rinehart and Winston, 1965.

Wertheimer, M., *Productive Thinking*, Harper, New York, 1945.

Whitfield, P. R., 'Environment and Engineering', and 'Environment: Its Improvement and Encouragement', in Gregory, S. A. (ed.), *Creativity and Innovation in Engineering*, Butterworths, 1972.

Whiting, C. S., *Creative Thinking*, Reinhold, New York, 1958.

Whittle, F., James Clayton Lecture: 'Early History of the Whittle Jet Propulsion Gas Turbine', *Proceedings of the Institution of Mechanical Engineers*, Vol. 152, 1945, pp. 419–35.

'Jet': *The Story of a Pioneer*, Frederick Muller, 1953.

Index

More about Penguins and Pelicans

Penguinews, which appears every month, contains details of all the new books issued by Penguins as they are published. From time to time it is supplemented by *Penguins in Print*, which is a complete list of all titles available. (There are some five thousand of these.)

A specimen copy of *Penguinews* will be sent to you free on request. For a year's issues (including the complete lists) please send 50p if you live in the British Isles, or 75p if you live elsewhere. Just write to Dept EP, Penguin Books Ltd, Harmondsworth, Middlesex, enclosing a cheque or postal order, and your name will be added to the mailing list.

In the U.S.A.: For a complete list of books available from Penguin in the United States write to Dept CS, Penguin Books Inc., 7110 Ambassador Road, Baltimore, Maryland 21207.

In Canada: For a complete list of books available from Penguin in Canada write to Penguin Books Canada Ltd, 41 Steelcase Road West, Markham, Ontario.

Management Decisions and the Role of Forecasting

Edited by James Morell

Forecasting in business, though notably more
sophisticated than crystal-gazing, is still an art rather than
a science because of the imperfection of past statistics and
our continuing ignorance of the future. The business
wizard of today is the man who can, as scientifically as
possible, lessen the uncertainties of the future and pinpoint
the risks, whether at company or national level.

This Pelican is a guide, prepared by a specialist of more
than twenty years' experience, to business forecasting in all
its aspects and the role it fulfils for management. A team of
economists engaged on the production of *Framework
Forecasts* contribute articles on the national economy, the
balance of payments and future government policy, trends
in major industries, public spending and interest rates and,
at the more workaday level of the individual company,
show how forecasts are made of costs, prices, sales and
profits.

With the aid of forty charts the book explains the
different techniques for forecasting, the basic information
required, and the ways in which findings can be
interpreted.

Business Adventures

John Brooks

John Brooks is famous for his business commentaries in the *New Yorker*. To those who think that modern business and finance lack drama and adventure his irreverent and immensely witty and informative reportage will come as a revelation. In these amusing and vivid essays he delves deeply into what goes on behind the scenes in Wall Street. To whet the reader's appetite we need only mention the remarkable success story of *Xerox Xerox Xerox Xerox* or, in *One Free Bite*, a battle in the courts between rival manufacturers of space suits.

'. . . a relaxed, witty and ironic writer, but the agony of the pound has inspired him to something more like a tragedy. As narrative, you may take my word for it that it is gripping stuff; and as explanation, it is unusually lucid' – *Guardian*

'. . . his articles are a delight to read. He parades a series of wildly funny situations before the reader – all of them with serious implications for the business world' – *New Society*

'. . . fascinating reading . . .' – *Scotsman*

Not for sale in the U.S.A. or Canada

Management and Machiavelli

Antony Jay

'The new science of management is in fact only a continuation of the old art of government.'

It is Antony Jay's entertaining contention that history repeats itself . . . in the modern business corporation, where kings, courtiers, barons, and serfs struggle as ruthlessly for power as ever they did in the Middle Ages or the Renaissance; that management, being more concerned with men than with machines, markets, products, or processes, can only be properly understood in political terms. Machiavelli may be a better guide than Drucker.

'An extremely stimulating and original book. It deserves a wide readership and points the way to a new field of research' – C. Northcote Parkinson in the *Spectator*

'An exciting and critical discourse on top management ideology and practice in the modern British corporation . . . a book to read' – D. F. Berry in the *Financial Times*

'Mr Jay writes well, has read widely and, like the first-rate TV producer he is, crackles with ideas' – *New Statesman*

'No ambitious young business school graduate aiming at the top can afford to be without this copy of who's-who-on-corporate-Olympus' – John Cockcroft in the *Daily Telegraph*

Not for sale in the U.S.A.

Corporation Man

Antony Jay

It has been said that, to be successful, a revolution must be managed by a group of men no larger than a football team. In *Corporation Man*, Antony Jay shows us why, but in the context of the modern business corporation.

Enlisting the aid of the new work being done in the behavioural sciences, he analyses the behaviour of companies and comes out with a set of conclusions that make *Corporation Man* a fitting companion to the work of C. Northcote Parkinson on the bookshelves of the thinking businessman. The basic unit of management is, or should be, the 'ten-Group', a group of about ten men engaged on the same task. This group, the lineal descendant of the primeval hunting-band, balances the individuality necessary for generating new ideas with the support and comradeship required for developing them. From here he goes on to the complexities of staff and line management, conglomerates and multinationals, producing some fertile new ideas about the proper running of a business.

Not for sale in the U.S.A.